TALES FROM THE SECRET FOOTBALLER

To Shakeel, my friend and TSF Chairman,
for all his support and encouragement.

TALES FROM THE SECRET FOOTBALLER

He's back. And this time
he's brought his mates.

First published in 2013 by Guardian Books, Kings Place,
90 York Way, London N1 9GU and Faber and Faber Ltd,
Bloomsbury House, 74–77 Great Russell Street,
London WC1B 3DA

This paperback edition first published 2014

2 4 6 8 10 9 7 5 3 1

A CIP catalogue record for this book is available
from the British Library

ISBN 978-1-783-35033-9

Text design by seagulls.net
Cover design by Mark Ecob

Printed and bound in Great Britain by
CPI Group (UK) Ltd, Croydon CR0 4YY

FSC
www.fsc.org
MIX
Paper from
responsible sources
FSC® C101712

CONTENTS

I ain't gonna work on Maggie's farm no more
No, I ain't gonna work on Maggie's farm no more
Well, I wake in the morning
Fold my hands and pray for rain
I got a head full of ideas
That are drivin' me insane
It's a shame the way she makes me scrub the floor
I ain't gonna work on Maggie's farm no more

BOB DYLAN

MY HUSBAND, THE SECRET FOOTBALLER

Almost anything can happen in professional football: one moment a player is basking in the glory of a successful season, the next he is looking for a new club and realising that his world is a very small oyster. What makes each season fly by is that it is packed with incident.

The only thing my husband ever said with regard to his football career was that he was going to get to the top: he was going to play in the Premier League. He didn't care about being famous but he already recognised the by-products of being a successful footballer and he'd goad our friends when we were out together: "Your kids will have my name on the back of their shirts one day. They'll watch me on TV and call me uncle." He's always known how to rub people just hard enough that they'd back away from him.

At the club he still loves, and at which he spent much of his early career, he was hugely influential on the pitch: when he arrived they had nothing and when he left they were an established force in English football. And he isn't modest about that: if you ask him, he'll tell you exactly what he thinks about his own contribution to that success. He was so important to that club that they would send him out on to the pitch hobbling on occasions. There was one season in particular when I don't think he returned from a single game without an injury of some sort – a strapped ankle or a swollen thigh or cuts and bruises all over his face and body – but he never complained. He would say to me, "The best players get kicked. When I come home with no cuts on me, start worrying." Last season he came home with a 10in gash down his shin and passed out on our bed. At about 2 in the morning I felt the covers being pulled off me; it turned out he was making his way to the toilet and was dragging the duvet behind him because the blood had stuck his leg to it. He's ruined so many nice bedspreads down the years that I stopped buying them long ago.

A few years ago he spent a week in Leicester having a course of injections in his knee; they administered Rohypnol because the doctor needed him conscious for the procedure, but it was extremely painful. One day there was a knock at the door and I opened it to find him looking as if he'd been in a drunken fight. I laid him down on the sofa and his mobile phone rang. It said "Physio", so I answered it and a voice at the end of the line told me that the hospital had lost him and were doing everything they could to find him. I explained that he was with me and the physio told me to keep an eye on him and wait for the Rohypnol to wear off – which eventually it did. An hour later he walked into the kitchen, extremely groggy, complaining that his arm hurt. I pulled up his sleeve and he had the IV hanging out of his arm.

I remember once he had me in tears laughing while a doctor was trying to treat him: he was still in his kit as the doctor attempted to put 30 stitches into a cut above his eye. The doctor had said that he had wanted to do the procedure under general anaesthetic but then he made the mistake of saying that only rugby players had so many stitches without general anaesthetic. My husband lost consciousness at least once but when it was finished he said, "There you go, doc. My eye is stitched up and all the rugby players still wish they'd been footballers, so what are you going to tell the next one that comes in here?" You have to know how to take him because everything is a challenge, and so long as it is him who instigates it there is nothing that he can't do.

Neither of us would miss the damage that football has done to his body, though. It is bad enough watching him lose a match and the mood that it puts him in, but when he can't play at all because of an injury the atmosphere in the house really isn't pleasant.

He has been recognised by his peers and the clubs that he has played for. He has had some success and won trophies, but when he looks back and adds up the time that he spent playing compared with where he might be now if he'd used his head instead of his feet, I know that he feels he made the wrong decision. He could be more respected, wealthier and, above all, happier. He feels that he's wasted the last 15 years of his life. It may seem ungrateful to say so, but I don't disagree.

Neither of us knew exactly what was going to happen once he started to play football for a living, but after three or four years he definitely changed. He became withdrawn. At first I thought it was because he was so focused, but years later, when I knew he wasn't taking his football so seriously any more, he remained the same. He'd crossed over into another personality and most of the time there wasn't any way to reach him.

Football, like life, can sometimes be absurd; a person might think that he is getting everything he could ever want, only to find out that it means nothing. When my husband got to the Premier League he didn't know why he was in the game any more: he desperately wanted to play football at the highest level and when he achieved that there was nowhere else to go. Simply surviving in the Premier League is enough for a lot of clubs – for the players, the managers, the fans and certainly the owners – but that was completely alien to him. I don't think he had seen success defined in those terms before and he was angered by it. It's easy to say now, but that was when he should have retired. He'd reached his goal; he had no plan thereafter.

When I look back to when I first met him, I recall that he had a picture of Kurt Cobain in his bedroom: it showed the Nirvana frontman slumped against the stage after a gig, sobbing uncontrollably, as if he had nothing left to give and nowhere left to go. At the time it was just a cool picture of a hugely influential person, so I never really asked him about it.

But a few years ago an article that had been cut out of a newspaper appeared on our fridge door. It told the story of what happened immediately after Pep Guardiola's Barcelona won the Fifa Club World Cup, to complete a clean sweep of every competition they had entered. Halfway through the article, somebody had picked out a quote in yellow high-lighter. Guardiola's assistant, Tito Vilanova, had finally tracked the manager down; Guardiola, in tears, turned to him and said, "Where are we supposed to go from here?"

It's a question I hear a lot nowadays.

Mrs TSF

INTRODUCTION

The last couple of years have been a monumental struggle.
I've had fights with ex-clubs, ex-managers and new chair-
men, while at the same time wrestling with the fact that the
end of my playing career is just around the corner. I am rela-
tively young and could play on for a few more seasons, but it
is time to do something else. My next step, if I can summon
the strength to take it, is important for a number of reasons.
It is important financially, of course, but more than that it
is important to me mentally because my biggest struggle
recently has been with myself. Despite the drugs I take for
the depression that has plagued me for more than a decade,
it has become increasingly difficult to get through the day
without thinking, "What's the fucking point?"

And I know that it will be difficult to move on, not
because I'll miss playing football particularly but because
other people don't want me to. I have been in business
meetings talking about exciting projects and creative ideas
that involve websites, inventions, manufacturing and so
on, and every time it's the same: whether I'm talking to an

investor, a chief executive or a designer, within 10 minutes the conversation turns to football and that makes me feel like the sad clown, someone who is only there for the amusement of everybody else. That's why I originally decided that if I was going to talk about football, it was going to be on my terms. If people found what I had to say interesting, then fine; if not, no problem. That was how The Secret Footballer was born.

As TSF, I've loved the freedom I've had to reveal how the "beautiful game" really works. I'll be doing more of that in this book. I don't want to give you a cheesy line but some of it you really wouldn't hear anywhere else.

I can't talk about football without telling you a little bit about my life, however: where I came from and how I came to be ... *different*, as some people would put it. That's a footballer's euphemism for "a cock" and a manager's polite way of telling my agent that he thinks I'm a trouble-maker who wouldn't fit into his team. Some of the things that I have done during my time as a footballer I am not proud of, but as I've admitted from day one, I am not whiter than white.

I can't deny that this life has been a real eye-opener. I have experienced every emotion that a footballer can experience in more than 10 years of playing professionally, and heard more than a few fantastic stories too. Some of them still make me cry with laughter whenever I hear them. I've managed to blackmail some of the players involved into telling them again for this book, and I hope you enjoy them as much as I do. Fair play to them for letting me use their stories, because if there's one thing I have learned from my years in the game, getting a footballer to play ball is by no means a given. As with my own tales, I've changed or fudged a few details here and there to protect the guilty.

Not all the stories are about what happens on the pitch; they just happen to concern footballers in various situations. Some of them are funny and some of them are extremely sad, and depending on the stereotype that you have in your head you may laugh at the sad ones and cry at the funny ones. My favourite story is about a very expensive yacht hanging by its stern from the side of a marina: whenever I picture that it makes me laugh, and the players who were involved tell it so enthusiastically, too.

This book is also about my quest for some kind of meaning as I search for my next job. I am finding it very hard to throw my energy into something simply for the money or as a way to keep busy. I want more than that. As you'll know if you've read my columns, many of them reflect where I am in my life at a given moment. I hope you'll be interested in seeing how some of my other writing came about, whether it was after a chance meeting with a quantum physicist in a coffee shop or a random dream brought about by a period of cold turkey.

Finally, I'll be updating you about what has happened since the summer of 2012, when my first book, I Am The Secret Footballer, was published. My life has a habit of heading off at unimaginable speeds in unpredictable directions just as I think I'm finally about to catch my breath.

In 2012 I signed a deal that I was not expecting. The club involved had suddenly lost a player in circumstances I can't go into and wanted me to fill the void until he got himself out of his spot of bother. I didn't want to sign, if the truth be told, but as well as being very persuasive, the owners are also very good friends of mine. One thing led to another and the enjoyment that I got from the following season was unlike anything I had experienced for years. For the briefest of moments I remembered why I loved football.

Before I signed I called a friend at a big boot manufacturer who sent me the latest pair of his company's horrifically coloured plastic monstrosities. He's always been good to me, even though these days nobody gives a shit what boots I wear, in particular the mums who used to ask me every five minutes because their sons wanted the same. But once I had them the familiarity was overwhelming – the smell, the touch, the ritual of slipping them on and pulling the laces tight and the pressure around the foot as the leather fell in on itself. It just felt right. "Just when I thought I was out," I said to myself, "they pull me back in."

PART ONE
A GAME OF
TWO HALVES

What I'll miss about my life as a footballer
– and what I'll be glad to see the back of

IT'S NOT ABOUT THE MONEY

In the last few years I have played against two former clubs. In one match I left the field to the fans singing my name; in the other I barely made it out of the stadium. It was another example of football's ability to throw up uncomfortable scenarios for everyone involved: no matter what team you support or which team you play for, sooner or later you will have to face people with whom you have history. The shit that I have had to deal with recently has been relentless.

As I look back on my career, I occasionally reflect that it might have been a good idea to keep my mouth shut when slating various people, clubs or fans, but that wouldn't have been me and there is nothing worse than a kiss-arse in football. I'd certainly be wealthier if I was like that but I can almost guarantee that I'd have had a breakdown by now. No, I only know how to be myself.

I knew there would be uncomfortable games to play because I have pissed people off over the years. Sometimes it was deliberately, sometimes unintentionally – but the result is always the same. Lots of players say things that annoy other people without thinking about how they will deal with it in real life rather than from the safety of their Twitter accounts. Eventually you find yourself playing away from home with everything stacked against you and the fans baying for your blood, and it isn't pleasant.

A while ago, and not for the first time in my career, my position at the club I was playing for became untenable. There were two reasons. Firstly, I was in the grip of depression to the point that I simply could not function, either off or on the pitch. Eventually I made the decision to inform my manager that he would have to drop me; unfortunately, he decided to give me one last chance. I had to appreciate what he was trying to do but he got it completely wrong, and therein lies the fundamental difference between managers who are successful and managers who are not. A successful manager will always do what he thinks is right for the team, not the individual. Don't get me wrong: he'll make sure that the player is OK – but if he can't perform, he won't play.

Secondly, the club was in financial trouble and owed its players a lot of money. They owed me so much that I thought I was going to lose my house. Shit happens; I don't want sympathy and I've never asked for it because I have faith in my ability to make sure that things work out for the best. This saga dragged on for more than a year, with false promises of payments that were followed by yet more contract negotiation and the signing of even more paperwork. Somewhere an entire forest must have given its life in A4 just for me to sign countless pieces of paper that seemingly meant bugger-all.

Meanwhile, the fans were being repeatedly told that if the players who were owed money insisted on being paid, the club would have to go into liquidation. So they were on at us, standing outside the training ground and shouting profanities as we drove through the gates and walked to the changing rooms. People can be very brave from a distance. One day something just flipped inside me and I walked over to have it out with a couple of them. After we'd all shaken hands, they told me that the survival of their football club was more important than any one person. I should be a "hero", as they put it, and save the club by forgetting about the money I was owed.

"What matters more to you, mate?" I asked one of them. "Your family or this football club?"

He didn't hesitate. "My family," he said.

"Same here," I said. "I need that money to make sure that my family have a home to live in, so I'm afraid I can't simply waive that money, because I wouldn't be able to support them, would I? How am I going to pay my mortgage? It wouldn't be very responsible of me to go home and tell my wife and children that I've forfeited a huge amount of money and we've lost our house but it's all right because some football club that we've got no real affinity for is going to get away with not paying its debts."

There was silence all round and the men looked very unsure of themselves. I didn't want to embarrass them; I just wanted to put a side of the story across that I knew they were not being told. The conversation went on and it became clear that he and his friend were typical of a lot of fans. They don't really understand the politics of the situations that they get so impassioned about, and they care little for the players in the middle of them because as far as they are concerned, every footballer is a millionaire, isn't he? I didn't tell them about all the considerations that I had to make: the fact that this money was needed because I had a huge tax bill to pay; the fact that the bank was threatening to repossess my house. To all intents and purposes, I was just a greedy footballer.

Fans can be very selective about what they decide to believe but, in fairness to them, in this case there had been a huge amount of bollocks written about the financial plight of this club. There had been even more crap put into the public domain by the owners, would-be owners and previous owners. In fact the only faction who had kept their counsel had been the players. In hindsight, maybe that was a problem for the fans, but sometimes you're damned if you do and damned if you don't. The people who were responsible for plunging the club into its dire financial situation were long gone and the players were being held accountable for abuses that extended back to before most of them had even arrived at the club. It was crazy.

To make things worse, that particular summer finding another club was tough, if not impossible, for me. Some of the younger players were walking straight into new contracts at other big clubs on good money; this meant that they could afford to wait for what they were owed and sign the deferral contracts that the club was pushing them into. My situation was slightly different, as I found out from my agent and an ex-manager that I had remained friends with.

In the market, my name had been absolutely slaughtered by another ex-manager of mine, whom I despise. The feeling is clearly mutual, given that every phone call that my agent made yielded the same response: "We know he's a decent player but we've been warned off him – he's trouble." He knew the situation at my current club was dire; he also hated the club for reasons that we won't go into but must have had a bearing on his decision to warn every manager that he could think of not to sign me. The result was that I became trapped in limbo: I couldn't get a new club because my name was being abused by a cantankerous old fuck, and I couldn't get out of the club I was currently at because they wouldn't pay me what they owed me. The fans were getting angrier and angrier. Something had to give.

• • •

In the event, it was me – I left the club without getting my money. The season was about to start and if I was going to find a club then I'd have to leave before I became a registered player. I was forced to gamble that my negotiating position would not be weakened by the fact that I wasn't in the building any more. That had been my concern from day one, and the club knew it.

I had signed the first deferral contract some six months earlier, and I had been told to expect the money in six months' time. That meant six months with no income and nothing left to sell, while trying to pay a mortgage of £16,000 a month and a tax bill of hundreds of thousands, not counting fines for late payment.

Now we were being asked to defer what we were owed again, which would have meant certain bankruptcy. I was forced to tell them that I wasn't signing; I had to hang my hat on the fact that they owed me a lot of money. That way I would have some sort of asset when I turned up at the bank to ask for a new mortgage. To all intents and purposes, the club now had to pay me whether it had the money or not. Almost overnight the whole thing became a game of Russian roulette.

The Professional Footballers' Association was a disgrace throughout the entire ordeal, by the way. It was spooked from day one by this case and it ran a mile. When football takes its gloves off and the going gets tough, it seems the PFA does not give a shit about anybody unless they are an elite player at a top club. We had next to no help or contact, no advice or guidance, and the players were left to fend for themselves. The situation was so complicated that it almost appeared as if everyone who was not directly involved simply stood back to see who would blink first.

Luckily I did find a club – a big club – and the signing-on fee that I negotiated was enough to keep the house safe, for a while at least. Even so, when the game against my former team came around my head was all over the place. At one point I thought about asking the manager to leave me out, but that isn't me and I dismissed the idea almost as soon as it came to me. I'm not a coward, never have been, but I knew it would be bad – and so it proved.

When my name was read out, the boos that rang around the ground were deafening. The game completely passed me by and the abuse became worse until finally it was over. I came in from the game and got changed before leaving the ground and heading home, but I felt and still feel such resentment for those fans and that club. No wonder nearly every footballer feels that fans are completely clueless. It is true that this bunch were deceived by a lot of conflicting stories, but whenever any doubt remained in their minds, they took the easy option and turned on the players.

Then a set of very curious circumstances came about. First the bank rang to say that there had been an oversight on my mortgage and that I had been overpaying for two years. Rather than £16,000 a month, I should have been giving them £10,500. There was no apology; in fact the woman assigned to my case almost seemed to be waiting for a "thank you". In the event she got a different two words out of me and we haven't spoken since.

The second stroke of luck came when the owner of my new club rang me the day after the game. "Look," he said. "I don't know whether you can use this in your dealings with your old club as a negotiating point, but when the fans started singing that song about you, their chairman stood up in the directors' box and joined in."

"You're joking!" I said.

"No, mate," he said. "I had to ask him to sit down while reminding him that you're one of our players and that he should stop acting like a 10-year-old and show some respect."

"Good for you, mate. Quite right too," I said.

"Yeah, but when he sat down he turned to me and said, 'Yeah but it's only [The Secret Footballer] – he deserves it.'"

There was silence at both ends for what felt like a minute but was probably only 10 seconds or so. Eventually I cobbled some words together.

"Say again, mate," I said. "What did he say exactly?"

He told me again and I lost it. There was a lot of swearing, mainly from me, and further requests for a full account of what had taken place just to make sure that I was hearing this right. I rang off and sat in silence for an hour or so, thinking about the situation. The worst thing to do when you're angry is react immediately; these days I try to digest the information and work out the next move. That's something I've learned to do over the years from friends who run successful businesses, even if it is against my nature. I decided that the first call should be to my agent, who had been dealing with this situation alongside me. I told him the story, he rang our lawyers – and all hell broke loose. The lawyers had plenty of ideas and seemed very excited by this latest development. What, they asked, did I want to do?

"You know what?" I said. "For months I've been bending over backwards for them. I've deferred payments that were due for fucking months, years even, sold everything I own, put my house up for sale, and this is the thanks I get? Ring that chairman and tell him to stick his contract right up his arse." (He was *still* hoping that I would agree to defer payment.) "Tell him I don't want to help him and he'll have done all this work for nothing. I don't even want the money any more; it's not even about the money – I just want to see him fail. I want to see what he has to say to the fans after he fails, after all his bullshit about him being the saviour of the club."

I was absolutely spitting feathers at this point. Despite the drugs, I can still be a spiteful bastard when the mood takes me.

"This is the important bit," I continued. "Tell him that tomorrow morning every single newspaper in the country is going to carry the story of what he said in the directors' box at the weekend, and everybody will know that the reason the club failed is that he couldn't keep his mouth shut and stop himself from giving it the big one in front of his mates. Tell him that my owner is going to allow the papers to use him as a named source."

The last bit was an outright lie, but so far as the rest of it was concerned I was deadly serious.

Twenty minutes later the lawyer phoned back.

"The chairman at the club has denied all knowledge of your accusations. He did say that he had got carried away and maybe said some things that he shouldn't have in the heat of the moment, but that's all."

"Right," I said. "So did he or didn't he say it?"

He ignored me.

"Furthermore, he wanted me to tell you that he thinks you're a great player and that he appreciates everything you've done in helping him to save the club. He understands the financial sacrifice that you and the other players have made.

He has asked me to apologise to you for getting carried away and has once again relayed to me in the strongest possible terms that the club has no money and will not survive unless all the players sign the paperwork that was emailed to them asking to defer payments once again."

"Well, that's the situation, then, isn't it?" I said. "Tell him that he's just pissed away two years of his life, because I'm not signing it. I want to see him fail and I want everybody to know that the reason the club failed is because of what he said in that directors' box. Before the week is out I'll have his name and the comments that he made in every paper in the country, just as the club did to me when they were trying to point the finger of blame at the high earners."

"One minute," said the lawyer. "It is my legal obligation to tell you that you ought to sign the deferral contract if you are to stand any chance of receiving any of the money that is owed to you."

"I hear you," I said, "and I know you hear me. It isn't even about the money any more because he has made it personal. So please go back to him and tell him I'm not signing the deferral contract. You know me. You know how serious I can be. I'm deadly serious."

Thirty minutes later the phone rang again.

"Are you alone and sitting down?" the lawyer said.

I wasn't. "Yes," I lied.

"I've just had a call from the representatives of the club," he said. "They have asked me to pass on their full and frank apologies once more and have also instructed me to inform you that they'd like to offer you a full settlement of the outstanding amount."

"You're joking," I said.

"No," came the reply. "I'm not joking. However, there is a condition."

"Right," I said. "What's the condition?"

"For God's sake keep the chairman's name out of the papers. I know you and they know you and we're all a bit worried at the minute. You haven't called any journalists yet, have you?"

"No," I said, which was another lie. Well, when in Rome ...

Let me give you an idea of what a monumental break-through this was. The club had preached, very publicly, that it had absolutely no money and that the situation was dire. It had even asked the fans to contribute huge amounts of money to a fund to save it. Clearly that was bullshit. The problem is that at these murky levels of negotiation you have to juggle so many factors in order to get a result, and you have to hold your nerve. My strength is that I'll hold my nerve to the point that it's to everyone's detriment, even mine. So long as you're prepared to do that you'll always get to the truth; whether that truth helps your situation or not is another matter.

But I also had to do something that didn't sit well with me. I'm OK fighting against authority figures, but I do have a conscience when it comes to selling my own grandma down the river. In this case, however, I had to make an exception. Many of my former team-mates who were in the same situation as me had called to ask what I was going to do (they always do that, but only because I pronounce the t's in words when I speak), and I told them not just that the deferral contract was our best chance of getting paid, but that I had already signed it. It isn't personal – it's just business as they say. As much as I enjoy the company of some of those lads, my responsibility is, as I've already said, to my family. And this was a desperate situation: the TSF household was on the line.

So we finally settled, I accepted the chairman's apology and I also agreed to keep his name out of the papers. And do you know where all that money went? HMRC. And it still wasn't enough to pay the bill.

And so ended one of the most depressing sagas of my life. I never wanted things to turn out this way; I just wanted to play football. But sometimes circumstances conspire against you and take that simple pleasure out of your hands; then you can either piss and moan that your luck is crap or you can stand up and fight and hope that people see the truth of the situation.

They still hate me at that club, and that's fine. I could do without it but I'm a big boy and I'll live with it. But they should know that if I hadn't got the rest of the squad to sign the deferral contracts, they'd have no football club to support and no seat from which to abuse me.

OK, IT'S ABOUT THE MONEY

Football is changing, though you probably don't need me to point that out. The deals that are being put together are incredible. The American business magazine Forbes now has Real Madrid ahead of Manchester United as the world's most valuable football club, with an estimated worth of $3.3bn to United's $3.165bn. That's despite the fact that independent analysis suggests that United have more than twice as many overseas followers as Madrid.

The way Madrid have achieved this is a testament to the power of their brand. Together with Barcelona, Madrid now account for half of the $750m TV rights in Spain. And thanks to years of those lucrative TV deals, Madrid have finally been able to start work on a $320m modernisation of their famous stadium that, when finished in 2018, is expected to push matchday revenues past $220m a year.

The most amazing part of president Florentino Pérez's strategy, however, is the way he has been able to persuade the world's best talent to meet him halfway financially if they want to play for Madrid. And herein lies a clue to the recent reports of disharmony among some of Madrid's biggest stars.

Since Pérez came to power, he has managed to convince every player who has followed him to part with half of his off-field earnings. That's every sponsorship deal, every shirt sale and every endorsement that, as Pérez sees it, comes from piggy-backing on the famous name of Real Madrid.

So when you hear talk of an £85m transfer fee for the supremely talented Gareth Bale, don't be taken in. Yes, it is a real transfer fee but it won't be handed over to Spurs all at once. In fact, not many clubs hand over the full amount up front. Real Madrid will look to spread the payments over the length of Bale's contract. Once Bale is in the building, however, his contract starts in earnest and half of his off-field revenue will come to Madrid. In essence, the proceeds from Gareth Bale's own commercial activity will pay for his own transfer. You have to hand it to Pérez – it is a quite sensational business model.

How time flies when you're raking in the cash. It was back in 2002 that Manchester United signed a 13-year sponsorship deal with Nike worth £303m, a deal that also included a 50 per cent profit split from all merchandise sold. Although the current deal doesn't expire until 2015, both parties have already entered an exclusive renegotiation period.

The new figure, still being wrangled over, is said to be close to £1bn for a new 10-year merchandising and sponsorship deal.

Pushing the numbers north is the name of the game and in the last couple of years sports manufacturers and football clubs have adopted new ways of leveraging their combined potential.

Despite the emergence of Barcelona and the ever-present power of Real Madrid, Manchester United remains one of the world's most recognisable and valuable sporting brands, a fact emphasised by last season's announcement of a seven-year sponsorship deal with Chevrolet worth £357m. This deal was so extraordinary that it prompted the club to buy itself out of an existing training kit sponsorship deal with DHL. In fact, it was so extraordinary that 48 hours after it was announced, Chevrolet's parent company General Motors sacked the man behind it, Joel Ewanick, after it was revealed that GM would be paying more than twice as much as current shirt sponsor Aon.

Putting that embarrassment aside, however, United's ability to profit from its brand remains unparalleled in the history of British football. Manchester United the brand is as rampant as its team was in the Premier League last season; in 2012 the club opened an office in Hong Kong and announced that staff costs had risen to £40.3m "primarily due to growth in commercial headcount".

With more commercial staff comes an ever-increasing amount of commercial deals: £1.3m due to their players being selected for Euro 2012; and, as a result of Old Trafford being an Olympic venue, a rise in matchday revenue to £109.1m. United's overall income rose to £363.2m over the year to 30 June 2013, while its debt has shrunk to a similar figure.

When people ask me where I think football, will eventually end up, I have to weigh up what I actually think will happen and how much abuse I can take once I give my answer. But with half a dozen clubs in each top European league all chasing the same commercial success, I'm afraid that when I look down the track the only thing that I can see coming is a speeding commercial freight train.

The glory of winning in battle still exists in football, but it is a glory that is increasingly driven by people in tinted-glass boxes wearing severe suits. I'm not saying that there is anything wrong with that for now. I am happy to follow football as long as what is being offered on the pitch is entertaining. But there will come a time when the only way to push financial figures skyward – particularly TV revenues – will be to play more matches against the top teams. And my guess is that this will lead to two things. First, the Champions League will temporarily revamp itself so that the top teams compete on a league basis in what were the knockout rounds. Then, when this approach fails, the top European clubs will reject Uefa, thrash out their own TV deals and create their own league – a league in which financial fair play rules do not exist and the Champions League is truly a league of the world's championship-winning clubs.

As my father often says when we are discussing the state of football around the family dining table: "It doesn't matter, son. One day it's all going to disappear up its own arse anyway." Not long from now, it will be difficult to argue with him.

• • •

In the summer I had a very interesting offer from a club that is also undergoing a huge shift towards ensuring that boxes are filled and as many seats as possible are pre-paid. As I was turning over the offer, the chairman asked to see me in his office. At first I politely declined, because when a player is weighing up which club to sign for, of all the things that need to be arranged and dealt with, talking to the chairman is never one of them. However, he was insistent and so I buckled, drove to the stadium, and met him in his office.

In that meeting he spelled out his vision for the club. It had a huge catchment area that it wasn't maximising, a great stadium with good facilities, heritage and, above all, potential. It was very well positioned because it was solvent, there was no debt to speak of and there were some huge local companies that were as yet untapped.

It sounded very promising but after about 20 minutes I thought we should get to the point.

"Why are you telling me all this?" I asked.

"Because we want you to be our ambassador," he said. "We want you to speak to these companies on our behalf; we want you to represent the club and sell it to the people and to the corporations that are here in the city. I want to bring you here because you can communicate. Your football will take care of itself – we know that and I'm not worried about that – but I want you for what you can do off the pitch."

There was a backhanded compliment in there somewhere, a fair amount of assumption and no shortage of balls on his part.

Every player's contract, no matter what level he plays at, stipulates that he must perform a certain amount of "club duties" each season; this might mean coaching kids at a school or visiting a hospital. On the whole, there is a lot of moaning and swapping among the squad, but the things get done and there is an understanding among the players that this is an important part of the job. I told the chairman that I had no problem carrying these duties out, and not just because it is in the contract but because I quite enjoy it. I personally think that clubs should visit the kids' hospital far more often than on the odd occasion at Christmas. It's good for everybody concerned.

However, there are companies that pay me for my time these days. They pay me to speak for them when they are trying to introduce a football club to a new product, they pay me finder's fees, and some of them pay me to come up with ideas as part of their advisory boards. I love it and have learned a lot from it. Football and business have never been more closely linked. In the Premier League it is raining cash, so much so that some players feel it's funny to lie down in piles of £50 notes or pretend to wipe their arses with them. Outside the Premiership the tie-ups aren't as big but they are definitely happening. It just takes a bit more ingenuity to extract the cash from the money men's wallets.

There were signs of this influx of money long ago, far from the FT and the business blogs. Ten years ago I was in Marbella with a club I used to play for. We were standing outside Sinatra's Bar in Puerto Banus watching the yachts come in and the Ferraris going round and round with no other purpose than to see who could make the most noise in front of the most people.

Our squad had taken over the corner that Sinatra's bar straddles and was in full flow when a huge, beautiful boat manoeuvred itself into a berth smack-bang outside. A red Ferrari was sat opposite on the quay, its engine running. Twenty seconds later a walkway swung around from the boat and landed on the concrete next to the car. Then a very purposeful man strode from the boat, jumped into the car and revved the engine for the reason I've just mentioned, before pulling all of 30 feet around the corner and stopping in front of our squad. Now that he was a little closer we realised that it was the chairman of a rival club, a man who had done very well in business and was not afraid to say so as publicly as possible.

He pointed to our striker and told him to get in. The pair sped away around the back of the bars before coming right round and pulling up next to the boat, into which they disappeared. Half an hour later our striker reappeared, a little shellshocked and a little more intoxicated.

Of course, we all wanted to know what had happened on the boat. One of our squad, who had been slumped against a wooden post, jumped up to find out – only to crack his head on a hanging basket and knock himself out. After we'd all taken it in turns to have our photo taken with him while he was in the recovery position, two girls came over and took him away for the rest of the weekend, though not before berating us for the way we were treating our friend. I naturally felt duty-bound to remind them that there are no friends in football, only acquaintances.

Despite all the excitement, I did manage to pursue my enquiries.

"It was weird," the striker said. "He just offered me £30,000 a week if I'd hand in a transfer request."

This was in the days before £100,000-a-week footballers, and £30,000 was a lot of money at our level.

In the end, the striker didn't make the move and his career suffered as a result, while that chairman lost a huge proportion of his wealth in the financial crash. But that was the moment that I first realised that money talks. These days we have players' wages and clubs' commercial deals pushed into our faces by a media that still expects us to disapprove – but that's progress, that's democracy, that's freedom of movement, that's capitalism, and these are the principles upon which our society is built. It is ridiculous to be outraged by somebody's good fortune in earning more money than someone else. Besides that, the product on offer is first class. It would be different if we were watching dross each week, but in the top leagues around Europe the standard has never been better and I, for one, love watching these players ply their trade.

Now, for the first time in my career, as I sat there in that chairman's office, I was being asked to reflect on a proposal that didn't just require me to play football. For the first time in a long time I had some real options.

Whatever happens at the end of this season, I have made a decision: for the first time in more than a decade of playing football, I'm going to do what I want to do – not what an agent advises me to do, not what a club wants me to do, not what popular opinion thinks I should do. Down the years I've listened to all those people, and do you know something? None of them have a clue what is right for me and most of them know less than I do. I've decided that I'm going to take my life back and the football world, the media, the banks and in particular HMRC can all go and fuck themselves. I ain't gonna work on Maggie's farm no more.

CHARITY BEGINS AT HOME

With all this money sloshing around professional football, it's hardly surprising that charities try to get a bit of it. Now, I'll admit that philanthropy that extends past my immediate family and friends is something that has been lacking in my life. I could make a million excuses, all of which can be destroyed by a picture of a kid starving to death on the TV. But when I made it to the Premier League I decided to find one charity that I could contribute to; after a bit of research I decided that I wanted to help an organisation based in India that performed simple eye operations on people who would otherwise go blind. The cost of the operation was £5 a time. For some reason helping people to see really appealed to me: nobody should go blind just because the money isn't there to prevent it. I donated £1,000 a month for four years. That's an awful lot of people who have had their eyesight saved, young and old, and I'm very happy about that.

At first I was inundated with pictures of smiling people who had benefited: each month a huge box would arrive with another picture of "Benny", who was now looking forward to a life of being able to do all the things his friends could. At first that was fine, but after about 2,000 of these letters all saying pretty much the same thing, I phoned the organisation and told them that with all the money it must be costing to pulp a rainforest every month, I'd rather they just carried out more operations. The letters duly ceased, so hopefully a few more people had their eyesight saved.

At one of my clubs the players decided to give their wives something to do by having them create a charity. This charity would raise money for organisations chosen by two wives each year. So all the money raised from golf events and dinners that usually went God knows where would now go to a cause chosen by whichever player's wife had been nominated to lead that year's fundraising.

One year my wife was chosen and she put forward a charity that helped children who had lost a parent at a young age. The charity helped to explain what had happened and what it meant for them. It was very moving: at one of the dinners, the two founders made a speech that had the whole room in tears. It was a fantastic organisation that really did make a difference for a lot of people. Four years earlier my wife had lost her father to a heart attack, and although she is a very strong woman, she had a young sister who didn't really understand what was going on. It was a difficult time for all of us and this charity was a great way of helping young kids, like my wife's sister, who were struggling to put the pieces together,

It was all going so well: lots of cash was being raised and people were enjoying the events that were being put on. From a standing start it had been fantastically successful in a short space of time. From memory, I think that the charities were each making well over £100,000 from their year's association.

But then the captain put his own wife up and the charities that were chosen were very difficult to get to the bottom of. People were complaining that when it was time to make a cheque out after they'd won an auction, they'd be given a strange company name. Something wasn't right. One very good friend who is pretty well off and has the colours of the club running through his veins rang me to complain.

"Mate, I won that Manchester United shirt the other night and the people have just been in touch to tell me to pay the money into a personal account."

"What's the name on the account?" I asked.

"You don't want to know," he said.

"Oh my God," I stammered. "You are joking, aren't you?"

The next day I went to some of the players and told them what was going on; they'd had the same phone calls. It turned out that this was our captain's testimonial year and the chairman had told him that the club would not be entertaining any testimonial requests because players were earning too much money these days and didn't need them (I guess nobody should be rich except him). He seemed to have forgotten that fans might actually want to show their appreciation for what had most certainly been a fantastic career.

This is one of the reasons the club fell apart. It can all be traced to that decision not to offer testimonials to long-serving players who had given their all. That was when the captain and his wife decided to make themselves beneficiaries of the yearly charity drive.

When the truth came out it hit the other players hard and the captain was ostracised in a way that I have never seen before or since. The trust of the players fell apart, the team spirit disintegrated, and the bond that we had was broken. From then on we could barely win a single match. It can all be tied to that moment. What a tragic way for that player to finish what had been a fantastic career.

I wish this was the only abuse of charitable spirit that I ever encountered in the game. But there is a League Two club that likes to cry wolf every other year or so by telling the press it is about to go bust unless it raises a certain figure: £50,000, £75,000 etc. Each time we read about it, a certain Premier League team rocks up and plays a prestigious friendly before buggering off again. As the ground's seats fill up, the buckets come out and the fans are encouraged to put their hands in their pockets ...

Just so you know, that club's manager is the highest paid in the division. By a mile.

Charity, as has often been said, begins at home. For some people it seems to end there, too.

THE JOKER IN THE PACK

I've been accused of being a cynic. Perhaps I am, though the last chapter may explain why I have a low opinion of some of my fellow footballers. But I still believe this sport has thrown up some genuine heroes. Take Paul Gascoigne.

When I was a kid Gascoigne was the best player I'd ever seen. My limited football knowledge meant that I couldn't work out why he was better than the others on the pitch, only that he was doing things that nobody else was doing – probably because they couldn't. But now I realise that I was watching the finest English player of his generation, of any generation; a player who for me is in the all-time top 10. I don't say that because he's now in a bad way; I say it because I know what I'm talking about. He was the complete player.

I remember as a kid watching his England debut against Denmark; as he walked down the side of the Wembley pitch with the rest of the England squad I shouted "Gazza!" as loud as I could and waved frantically. He turned and walked towards the stands until he saw me, then he stuck his thumbs up high over his head while wearing the widest, cheekiest grin you've ever seen. Jesus, he made my childhood in that one moment.

Everybody knows about Gazza's crazier stunts, and yes, he has his demons, but when you speak to the right people you uncover stories that put this man right on the edge of genius. I spoke to a few people who played with him at various points in his career and they all say the same thing – that he is the most talented and dedicated player they ever played with, somebody who was fiercely competitive yet had time for everybody.

A friend of mine who played with him at Rangers in the 90s has no shortage of stories about Gazza, and every anecdote, whether it's on the pitch or off, always ends with, "What a player, though, pal. Jesus Christ." By the time Gascoigne arrived at Rangers he'd already had one career-threatening injury with Tottenham and a semi-successful spell with former Italian giants Lazio, and some thought he was past his best, but my friend begs to differ. His stories are worth quoting in full.

"One day at Rangers," he recalls, "I was making the tea for Walter Smith and the other coaches. Outside the training ground a crowd had started to gather: before long there were 100 people, soon there were 500, and later still it was impossible to tell. I knocked on the door and Walter barked, 'Come in.' I entered with my head down, put the teas on the table and desperately tried not to look at anybody in the room, because as soon as you made eye contact you became the coaches' bitch for the day. I tried to scuttle off when Walter piped up: 'Hey, just a minute, pal! Who's that sitting there?' I looked up slowly, and peering out from behind a door was Paul Gascoigne. It was unbelievable – for us it was like having Zidane or Cruyff sat there. He was already a legend.

"Shortly after he arrived the fun and games began. He was desperately trying to get fitter so he was spending a lot of time with the physios and fitness coaches. When that happens, you form this bond that stays between you both until the player leaves the club. We were playing Hearts away and players would often get their cars driven to the hotel on the Friday ahead of the coach if they were going on somewhere when the game finished on Saturday evening – the same as at every club. Gazza would always ask the physio because they had such a good relationship. So he gives the physio his car keys and tells him he'll see him at the hotel later that evening. The physio heads off in Gazza's car, and no sooner has he driven out of the training ground gates than Paul takes out his mobile phone in the changing rooms and taps a number in. The next minute you can hear, 'Yeah, police please, operator ... Yeah, hello, I'd like to report my car stolen, please.' By now all the players are wired in to his phone call. 'Yeah, I've finished training and I've come outside to go home and it's gone.'

"After everybody had clicked what was going on and Gazza had given the police the make and model of his car, we set off for the game on the team bus. An hour into the journey, Gazza's phone rings. 'Hello, Mr Gascoigne, we've stopped your car heading eastbound on the M8 towards

Edinburgh. The man driving claims to know you – he says he's the Rangers physio.'

"Gazza looks up and everyone on the bus is crying with laughter. 'I'm on the team bus, mate,' says Gazza. 'I'm looking at the physio right now.' 'No problem, Mr Gascoigne – we'll arrest the man now and have your car returned,' says the officer at the other end of the line, and he hangs up.

"Two minutes later the phone goes once more. It's the policeman again. 'I'm sorry to bother you again, Mr Gascoigne, but the gentleman here is becoming quite upset now and has asked to speak to you. Would you mind?' The policeman passes his phone to the physio and just as he is about to make a tearful plea for his freedom the entire bus breaks out into uncontrollable laughter. Gazza sorted it all out and squared it with the police, who thought it was hilarious. They were just happy to be a part of one of Gazza's pranks. He was brilliant, mate, so good for team morale. The lads loved him – and what a player, mate. Jesus.

"It takes a genius to think of things like that – his brain just worked differently from everyone else's. It was always to make other people laugh. That's the thing about Gazza – it was always for someone else. He was the most selfless man I ever knew. One time he spent five hours in the hairdressers having his hair put into dreadlocks – five hours, man! He came strolling into the training ground and as soon as the lads saw him, that was it – people were on the floor killing themselves.

"Then Walter walked into the changing room wearing his meanest scowl; he took one look at Gazza and with his sternest voice told him to leave the training ground, go back to the hairdressers and shave his head immediately. So Gazza sends one of the kids to buy him a huge hat so he can sneak past the paps that were always waiting for him, and he leaves training to get a haircut. As soon as he leaves, Walter Smith bursts into laughter. He had that effect on people – you just couldn't help laughing.

"Another day he walked into training with all his fishing gear on. He loved fishing. He had everything: the stupid hat with all the flies attached, the waders, the jacket with pockets all over it, even a smoking pipe hanging out of his mouth. Under one arm he had his rod and under the other he had the most enormous fish I've ever seen. It looked like a fat eel; its head and tail were both touching the floor as it looped under his arm. He hadn't been fishing, he wasn't going fishing, he was just coming in for a normal day's training and he'd decided to get dressed up in his fishing gear first and go to the market early to buy a fish. It was just for banter. What a bloke he was – absolute legend.

"But I want people to know what he was like as a player, I want people to understand how good he was. People think they know Gazza and they think they know his game, but I'm telling you nobody has ever scratched the surface. If I was a coach with the FA, I'd be showing my midfielders videos of Gazza's best games all day long. He was just unplayable. In training he was so strong, when he had the ball you couldn't get it off him. And he was aggressive with it, too – not in a dirty way, but if you came up alongside him you'd get an arm across your chest and a shove to go with it, and this is all at top speed. Not many players can do that. And he'd still have the end product: a pass, a shot or a cross. I'd go in to nick the ball off him and it was like hitting a brick wall – you couldn't move him when he had the ball. He was just phenomenal.

"And he was fit, too. This is what people never gave him credit for. He was probably the fittest guy I ever played with. I don't think anybody knows this but he gave himself two hernias from overtraining in the gym. He had that little double chin and everyone assumed he was fat, but he was seriously ripped, with a ridiculous six-pack. He was in the gym almost every day, first person in and last person out. He was obsessed with being as fit as he possibly could be because his talent demanded it. I've never seen anybody work as hard as Gazza did to be a footballer.

"He was loved, too. The players loved him, the owners loved him, the fans loved him, he was adored everywhere he went, and I know that was also true at Ibrox. We had a seriously talented team and he strolled in and took over the place. Not many people do that without sowing the seeds for a little bit of jealousy, but he did, and he didn't do it by kissing people's arses. He did it by being himself. When Adidas would send him 10 huge boxes of their latest crap he'd walk it all down to the youth team changing rooms and say, 'There you go, lads, help yourselves.' He'd stay for hours after training to talk to the two old women who washed the kit at the training ground. What would he be talking to two old women about for hours on end? I have no idea, but they loved him.

"He had loads of time for everybody, even the paparazzi, who treated him like shit. When I got to Ibrox we never had paparazzi, but when Paul Gascoigne arrived we had 10 full-time photographers outside the training ground right up until the day he left. That was hard for him and I swear he was on the front and back pages of the Sun for about two years, but he was always himself and he still made time for them. And they loved him for it, on a human level, and not just because he was great fodder for them."

Now imagine how it must feel when one morning you wake up and all of that has suddenly stopped. I am not and never was the player that Paul Gascoigne was, but because of that I know I will never end up like him either.

MY DRUGS HELL

People sometimes ask me if there's a lot of drug-taking in football. Perhaps they can see traces of my misspent youth.

It is fair to say that in my late teens I could have gone either way. In my search for some kind of meaning to life, I wrote songs and shared joints with what I liked to refer to as "like-minded people". The truth of the matter was, most of them were deadbeats. It was a morale-crusher when my father pointed that out, but he was right nonetheless.

All the kids in our street played football from the moment we came home from school to when our parents came looking for us because it was time for bed. But as we got older our priorities changed: at 16, 17 and 18 we discovered other things, like women, music, alcohol and, in some cases, drugs.

I was good friends with one lad in particular in our street, despite the fact that he was a year younger and went to a different school. One of our favourite pastimes was playing Championship Manager while on massive booze marathons that lasted for two or three days during the summer months when our parents were away. That game always had the effect of making us want to play football for real, so when we could stare at the screen no longer we'd go outside and kick a ball back and forth.

Over time we got to marking each other's control and technique out of 10. Under the dim glow of a single orange street lamp in a lay-by in one corner of our street, the only thing that could be heard was the monotonous echo of a ball being kicked, followed by a number being called. Hours we were out there, and inevitably my control improved until eventually it became flawless.

When we'd had enough we'd lie down in the middle of the road – it was a quiet street – and look up at the stars before pondering the fundamental questions of humanity: where do we come from, where are we going, what are we going to do with our lives and how much bigger could our neighbour's tits get?

My schoolfriends didn't mix with his, which isn't to say that my school was superior. I had just been lucky when our classmates were drawn out of the hat – for some reason I had been lumped in with the intelligent kids, while he ... well, he hadn't. Because of that he was able to lay his hands on some very good Jamaican woodbine. The search for answers seems important when you're that age, even though you don't have the knowledge to talk about such things with any great authority. The marijuana was an eye-opener, for sure. Like a lot of people who smoke it, I felt as if I was on to something but I was also very aware that the downside of the drug meant that I really couldn't be bothered to do anything about it, on the rare occasions when either of us said something worth further thought in the cold light of day.

Like all relationships, however, ours had its peaks and troughs. We had both taken part-time jobs on the same industrial estate, but as each of us made new friends at work we didn't really bump into one another too often, until gradually we simply moved on. There were lots of people around my age at the firm I worked for, and many of them are still friends of mine to this day.

A couple of them told me that they went clubbing every weekend and asked me if I wanted to go with them. I'd never been before; in fact, I had barely been out of my own town. But I couldn't wait to go. Over the next couple of years I got into clubbing in a big way and became part of a hardcore group who would follow DJs all over the country.

We went everywhere: London, Sheffield, Manchester, Birmingham, Liverpool ... Everybody in our town who was seriously into house music and clubbing would travel the length and breadth of the country to watch the biggest names in clubland perform. And while where I lived every night out ended with a fight unless you had a doctor's note, I can honestly say that in the clubs that I went to I never once witnessed any trouble. Well, almost never. I do remember being at the Don Valley Stadium for Gatecrasher's Millennium Eve event when somebody climbed the rigging and stopped the show. When he eventually clambered down, somebody smacked him. I've phoned one of the lads I was with that night and he tells me that the incident happened while Judge Jules was playing, and although we were a long way from the stage and we couldn't be absolutely sure, we still told everybody that it was Judge Jules who hit him.

The reason there was no trouble is largely that alcohol played second fiddle to ecstasy. Ecstasy convinces you that everybody is your friend. If you're walking along and you accidentally bump into a stranger who also happens to be on the drug, the apology tends to take on a life of its own, to the point where you end up hugging and offering to meet up later.

That isn't to say that there wasn't the occasional unsavoury incident. On one outing to Gatecrasher in Sheffield, we made such good time that we decided to visit a pub not too far from the club. About 30 of us descended on a nice-enough looking establishment but it became clear almost immediately that we'd made a terrible misjudgment. It was crazy – 15 to 20 local heavies mixed in with 30 of the most brightly dressed teenagers you've ever seen. The whole place was a seething mass of Day-Glo. It was difficult to tell who'd won by the end, but I remember there being a sudden realisation in both camps that we were all in this pub together and no one had had a beer in the last 10 minutes. It was surreal – the fight just seemed to fizzle out and people began queueing at the bar to order drinks. And as the barmaid tried to serve one person, he'd say to her, "Oh, actually I think that bloke is before me, love," before pointing to somebody from the other group. It was ridiculous: by the time it ended a bloke that I'd bought a pint of Foster's for was so grateful that he offered to "sort anybody out" who gave us grief while we were in Sheffield.

Since then, studies have linked ecstasy to depression when taken on a regular basis. I don't remember experiencing any of the other side-effects, such as overheating, high blood pressure, irregular heartbeat and renal failure, but I do remember suffering from terrible jaw-clenching. By the end of the night I'd have the mother of all headaches and I would not be able to prise my jaw open. It got to the point where I was beginning to wear my teeth down through constant grinding. I am ashamed to say that my solution was to wrap a £1 coin in a £20 note before placing the package toward the back of my mouth on one side between the top and bottom molars. When the pill took effect, I'd involuntarily clamp down and that would prevent the grinding. This wasn't a piece of drug-takers' knowledge passed between revellers; I had in fact stumbled on this solution myself after spending about £20 on packets of Chewits at the Ministry of Sound in London. I thought I'd put one of the sweets into my mouth but it turned out to be a coin wrapped in a note, as I realised an hour later when it was still intact. There's nothing glamorous about drugs, but on the other hand it did keep my cab fare safe.

Ecstasy, in part, is dangerous because the pills are produced illegally – which means there is no way of knowing how strong they are, or what other substances they contain. One night at the Ministry of Sound, they took me to a void in which time had no meaning.

Armand Van Helden was playing. We'd gone to see him because he'd been a rising star in our world for some time but now he'd made it big thanks to a monster hit entitled U Don't Know Me. This was his big night. I remember him coming on – but nothing else. Afterwards I was told that I'd been holding on to an exposed RSJ for around nine hours. Not moving, certainly not dancing, just holding on. I thought I was having a great time.

The fun really began when I got home. I climbed into bed and shut my eyes, my ears ringing. I was freezing cold, though I put that down to spending hours travelling home in nothing more than a short-sleeved T-shirt. I pulled the sheets up to my nose but the shivering got worse. I grabbed another blanket out of the airing cupboard and doubled it over before laying it on the bed, but it had no effect.

At some point I became aware of something going on around the edges of the bed, even though I knew that I was the only person in the house. My eyes were closed but I had the feeling that they were open, like the feeling you have when you know you're dreaming, only in reverse.

The shivers subsided long enough for me to reach for the glass of water on the bedside cabinet. I rolled over and opened my eyes and there they were: a dozen or so hooded figures with what appeared to be tridents in their hands walking very slowly, heads bowed, around the bed. They were emerging out of the wall to my right and walking around the foot of the bed and up the other side before disappearing into the wall on the left. Ecstasy isn't known primarily as a hallucinogen and most people don't take it for that, but it has been known. Whatever strain of MDMA this new pill belonged to, it was clear that the "comedown" was horrific. I lay in that bed for four fucking hours watching those figures. I have a fairly high threshold where being scared out of my wits is concerned, but that was the scariest thing I've ever seen.

It went on so long that I began to have serious thoughts about why they were there and where they'd come from. Maybe they had been sent? Who by? Shouldn't they be chanting something? I couldn't see their faces but nevertheless their appearance gave the impression that they should be chanting. In my brain something clicked into place: they must have a message for me. Almost as soon as that thought came into my head they began a slow, rhythmic chanting. I couldn't make it out at first, but as soon as I shut my eyes the words became clearer. The first two were drawn out, in keeping with the slow pace of the figures making their way in step around the bed. But the last word was more definite. Although I still didn't know who had sent them, it was now clear what they were saying: "FEEEED YOOOOUR HEAD, FEEEED YOOOOUR HEAD, FEEEED YOOOOUR HEAD, FEEEED YOOOOUR HEAD, FEEEED YOOOOUR HEAD."

And it is this remnant of ecstasy that has haunted me ever since. I have recurring nightmares of different people who always bring me the same message: "Feed your head." I have them to this day and they can be very scary because in every one of them I am about to die before I shake myself awake. My anti-depressants were supposed to stop them, and for a while they did, but as soon as my body became used to the dose the dreams came back with a vengeance. I think I got off lightly: many of my fellow clubbers have been left very distant by their own experiences and one who completely overdid it had to go through electroconvulsive therapy.

That was the last time I ever took drugs without a doctor's prescription. But that doesn't mean I've lost all interest in ecstasy. A steady trickle of research seems to indicate that some strains of MDMA – far removed from anything you'd ever buy on the street – can benefit sufferers of depression. I'd like to see greater research into this and other banned substances in the hope that it might extend the treatments available to people like me. For decades the blanket prohibition on possession and distribution has held back research. I'm not talking about legalisation – that's ridiculous. What I am saying is that these substances should be fully researched in controlled environments.

Anyway, my drug-taking started with marijuana and ended with ecstasy, with nothing in between. After I became a footballer it was impossible to go clubbing, much as I enjoyed it. And besides, the scene was changing: the music had enjoyed its golden period and clubbers weren't just indulging in different strengths of ecstasy any more. There was a new drug, ketamine. It came with the worrying warning that vets used a form of it as a horse tranquiliser. And as if that wasn't disturbing enough, "Special K" had the ability to temporarily paralyse people who took it as a pill. It didn't seem suited to the club scene at all.

That scared the hell out of me and I was glad to have moved on in my life. But I think that on some level it is part of the human condition – the need to explore and experiment, the quest to discover and learn.

• • •

I had long finished with ecstasy by the time I became a footballer, although that didn't stop me from dealing drugs in my first year as a professional. A friend had given me eight Viagra tablets for my personal use – I had no idea where they came from or why he thought I needed them, and I had no intention of taking them – and I mentioned my haul in the changing rooms. That led to a severe bout of peer pressure that only ended when I sold all eight tablets to two older pros for £25 a pop, which was good money for me back then. Apparently they were very effective, although to this day I've never tried them myself.

I have, however, been prescribed a whole pharmacy's worth of other drugs.

In my first book I told how a newspaper reported that I had become addicted to methadone after taking some heavy-duty prescription medication to numb the pain of a bad injury. I do not know where that story originated but it was completely fabricated. However, a couple of years after that incident I injured the same ligaments again and had to go back to the same doctor in the Midlands. For the second time I would have a needle pushed the length of my ligaments so they could be flooded with sugar solution. And again I might end up in agony.

As I made my way to see the doc on the Monday I couldn't help thinking about the excruciating pain I'd endured during the first course of injections. Typically, an injury such as the one I had requires a minimum of three or four courses of injections before the ligament is strong enough to cope with a stringent rehab programme. The solution works by encouraging the ligament to stiffen almost immediately, to the point that new cells grow within a matter of days. There are many people, mainly surgeons, who dismiss this treatment, but trust me, it works. Many physios in the Premier League and beyond today routinely send their players for a course of these jabs for all manner of ligament injuries, especially rolled ankles.

The first time round, I made the rookie error of trying to speed up the process by forgoing the local anaesthetic that was supposed to numb the area around the ligament. I never made that mistake again. The needle that delivers the sugar solution is about six inches long and as thick as a kebab skewer. It is inserted and manoeuvred with so much force that it very often ends up bent at the base.

Even with the local anaesthetic, the process wasn't pain-free. Because the sugar solution injections are so intrusive, the injections that deliver the anaesthetic need to be incredibly effective, and that means that before treatment on the ligament has even begun, a patient has to endure a dozen extremely painful jabs around the area to make sure it is well and truly numbed.

I told the doc that I couldn't face going through all that again. But apparently the medical world had advanced since

I'd last visited, and the procedure could now be done under semi-conscious sedation. Rohypnol was on the scene.

Rohypnol has a bad image: it is a very dangerous drug in the wrong hands. You may remember that not too long ago it was in the papers every week. A person who takes it will experience a sedative effect that brings on muscle relaxation and amnesia, even though they remain conscious and able to communicate. The drug is odourless, colourless and tasteless, which makes it ideal for spiking drinks. This combination of factors, plus a street price of around £1 a pill, has led to its use in countless cases of what has become known as "date rape".

I'm not sure if Rohypnol is addictive but I do know that the NHS doesn't use it. As footballers we generally don't have our injuries dealt with by the NHS, however. Our clubs have very cosy relationships with private health practices and insurance companies.

So when I asked the doc if there was anything he could do so that I didn't have to go through the pain all over again, he told me that he could book me in as a day patient to have the procedure under Rohypnol. He explained that it was essential to use a drug that wouldn't knock the patient out entirely. When the sugar solution is injected it is important to flex the joint so that the ligament responds as it would under natural tension. In other words, if the patient were under full sedation, the ligament wouldn't react in the proper way and the patient wouldn't be able to tell the doctor if the ligament had stiffened as it was supposed to. As long as I was semi-conscious I'd be able to give valuable feedback.

The first time I had this treatment I woke with the aid of another drug that was injected into an intravenous line inserted into my hand. I had a dry mouth and blurred vision and I asked the doc if everything had gone according to plan. "Yes," came the reply. "No problems at all. I'll see you next week." But that wasn't enough for me. "How does the joint feel?" I asked. "Strong?" That's when the doc walked around the side of my bed, leaned down so his mouth was close to my ear and said, "Listen, we've just had this fucking conversation not five minutes ago and 10 minutes before that. I can't have it again. Everything's fine – see you next week." It's a powerful and scary drug, that Rohypnol.

There was just one problem: the feeling as the anaesthetist pushed the drug into my drip and up my arm was incredibly seductive – so seductive, in fact, that I persuaded the club physio that the injury wasn't fully healed and that another two rounds of treatment would probably do it. In the sterile room in which these procedures were carried out, there was a metal grate on the ceiling and as the drug was injected, the sharp edges of the grate became distressed and began to wobble. I liked to think of that steel grate as a gateway; I didn't know where I was going but wherever it was it felt amazing. As I was drifting off during the last time I had this procedure, I looked at the anaesthetist and said, "I fucking love that feeling," at which he bent down and whispered in my ear, "You're not supposed to say that, you twat."

In the end I was busted by the fact that it had become impossible to get any more solution into the ligament. As a result I now have an abnormally sized ligament in one leg and no feeling around the joint. I can actually pull hairs out of my leg very slowly without feeling anything at all. Because of that, the third time I injured the same ligament the only way I could tell whether it was damaged was to kick a wall while the physio watched to see how far the leg was bending in the wrong direction. I'd tell you that the diagnosis of major ligament injuries has moved on these days, but it hasn't. If it ain't broke, don't inject it.

• • •

I have written one column for the Guardian about drugs in football and I stand by the tone of it: namely, that there is not a huge drugs problem in our game. There are examples, of course, but it's not as if we're uncovering a drugs cheat every other week. But after the column went out I was contacted by an organisation representing cycling, which accused me of being blinkered and covering up my fellow professionals' drug abuse. Quite why they felt they knew more than me I'm not sure, and it riled me hugely. I didn't reply, but a year later, when Lance Armstrong was found to have cheated his way to seven Tour de France titles, I took enormous delight in sending an email back to my antagonists pointing out that people who throw stones in glass houses should be bloody careful that their own sport isn't a complete and utter global embarrassment before they do so. Arseholes.

But just as I was feeling smug, my wife asked me if I could remember a story from a club I used to play for. It had completely slipped my mind but as soon as she mentioned the player's name the whole episode came flooding back.

During one of my first seasons in the Premier League we signed a player for many millions of pounds. It was a strange signing for us: he didn't seem to fit and he didn't seem to bond. For some reason he made friends with the youth team players, even though he had been bought to play in the first team. He lasted no more than a year; I turned up to training one day to find that we'd somehow managed to sell him for a profit to a rival Premier League team. A few days later I received a strange phone call from our chief scout, asking me why I thought the club had sold him. "He didn't fit in?" I suggested. "He seemed to make friends with the youth team and seemed a bit lonely?"

"Yeah, that's exactly it," he replied. "Do the other lads think that too?"

"I think so," I said, "but nobody really cares, to be honest."

"OK," he said. "I'll speak to you later." I now realise that he was fishing – but what for?

A year later a couple of bizarre things happened within a few weeks of each other. First a journalist friend of mine rang to ask what I knew about the same player's cocaine habit; he mentioned another player, too. I said I didn't know anything about it at all – but now that he had told me about it, the call that I had received from the chief scout made sense. I told him what had happened in the past and he told me what had been happening recently. "He's been a naughty boy at his new club. He and [the other player] have been caught in a drugs test with cocaine in their systems."

It made complete sense now that somebody had put all the pieces together in front of me. The reason these stories don't come out is that these are young men who have made a mistake and the unofficial policy seems to be to clean them up rather than destroy their careers. It's difficult to know where to stand on that one, but I suppose that if I had to stick a flag in the sand I would probably come down on the side of the player. He deserves to be punished, but that can be done by banning him from playing for a while and fining him. I don't think there is a need to destroy his career by going public. Everybody makes mistakes, but I've always been grateful for a helping hand. The moment your father says, "I'm not angry, I'm just disappointed" – that's all you need sometimes.

However, the fun and games weren't over because two weeks later we played against this player's new team. Our former team-mate wasn't playing, though, and I don't think he was even in the squad. This was dressed up as a contractual agreement that stipulated that he couldn't play against his former team. I, and all my old team-mates from that club with whom I still speak, now realise that this was complete bullshit. The game was extremely ill-tempered, as if the manager of the opposition had told his players to be overly aggressive. It's inexplicable when you're on the pitch – you know something has kicked it off but you can't work out what. Sometimes it's a personal spat between two players where one has slept with the other's bit on the side, which then spreads throughout the team; or sometimes it's bad blood between two managers that spills over on to the pitch as all the idiots who like to crawl up the arses of their bosses go around kicking people. We won the game thanks to a very contentious goal but the bad blood was everywhere. As we walked off the pitch there was a hold-up to walk into the tunnel; I was at the front of the players and barged past the police and stewards, only to be confronted by the two managers and about a dozen coaches, with a couple of cops trying to separate everyone. The opposition manager was livid and was shouting at our own manager, "You knew, didn't ya? You fucking knew and you didn't say anything! You sold me a fucking cokehead!"

The argument carried on and at one point spilled into the boot room, which had a maximum capacity of about six people. I knew exactly which player they were talking about, of course, and by the time they'd finished so did everybody else. There was no doubt that the manager of the other team had told his players to kick us to pieces because, as he saw it, he'd been stitched up by one of his peers – but if you don't do your homework and you don't even come in to the training ground until Fridays ... well, that will happen, I'm afraid.

So the rumours that we hear sometimes turn out to be true. It does happen. I didn't want to believe it for a long time but I'm afraid that it's a reality of the game. I'm half inclined to email that cycling group back and apologise – but no. I hate cycling.

Top players who seem to be out of action for endless periods are major targets for the rumour-mongers. Their absence is usually blamed on a back injury – even the "experts" have no clue when it comes to back injuries – or a viral condition, because that could mean anything. The rumours work along the lines that the club has struck a deal with the governing bodies that the player will enter private rehab and serve a ban, so long as his name and offence is concealed. Why would the FA do that? Because the players are in the national team. They're great rumours, and I wish I had evidence for more of them, but if you pick any top player who has been out for a long time with an injury that isn't particularly clear, just ask yourself what's going on.

MESSING ABOUT

While we're on the subject of footballers behaving badly, I must pass on what has become known as the Boat Story. (We made that title up all by ourselves, by the way.)

I first met the player at the centre of it in the Premier League; he breezed into training on his first day and never looked back. His performances were fantastic and he quickly had both the fans and the players on his side. On that first day, he arrived in a beautiful purple leather jacket; it sounds awful, I know, but he wore it so well and the fact that it matched his sports car only added to his lively character. I liked him the moment he extended his hand to me and said, "Pleased to meet you, pal. Where are we going tonight?"

Since that day, we have been great friends. I'd do anything for him and I think that works the other way, too. He is one of the most charismatic, energetic and, above all, talented footballers I have ever played with or against. He doesn't know this, but his signing was exactly what I needed at the time. It isn't an exaggeration to say that the moment he walked through the door everybody at the club, staff and players alike, became re-energised about the task ahead. I love this guy and I am a better player and person for having met him when I did.

Below is a story he told me a few years ago; it remains, to this day, one of my favourite-ever anecdotes. As with all tales like this, it is tinged with a sense of what might have been: it could so easily have ended in tragedy. I have a perspective on stories like this. These situations always seem to end well when certain people are involved – that is to say, these sorts of things are pretty much par for the course for them. They never think that the worst will happen to them and because of that it never does. If it had been me at the centre of this story, I'm sure there would have been a very different outcome.

The season had just finished and my friend hadn't put a foot wrong. The fans loved him and he was the focal point of all the good things that the team was doing. He had even been called up to play for England – a reward for his league form and the culmination of his efforts to date. It was a tremendous honour and he loved being part of that England set-up; more importantly, he felt at home there. He was fit and strong and had earned the opportunity. His manager was pleased for him, too: he had believed in him from day one and had built a very good team around him.

But he needed the break: all footballers do. No matter how well you're playing, you need the summer to let your body recover. You don't realise how much effort goes into matches while you're mid-season: only when you stop and catch your breath do you realise that you are functioning on autopilot. It's good to stop, look back and see where you can improve, and it's tough to do that when the games are coming at you from all directions. But as much as my friend was looking forward to a rest, he was also looking forward to the next season. That's the sort of player he is. I think that's why some of our team-mates said he had ADHD.

He'd made a lot of friends at the club; the players were a great bunch to be around and as they'd just come off the back of a successful season they were still enjoying one another's company. They went out together to the local restaurants, played golf together and went to one another's houses for dinner.

While everybody at the club got on well, my friend had a couple of mates that he was perhaps a little closer to than the rest. At the start of that summer, probably around early May, when the season was drawing to a close, the three of them had bought a yacht, as you do. This 30ft Sunseeker was sleek and menacing, a real work of art; it had two bedrooms, a galley, and enough room at the front for two or three people to sunbathe comfortably. It was a beautiful thing, and they were looking forward to sailing it up and down the coast all summer long. I'll let my friend tell you what happened there-after – it's only fair.

"For the first week or so we were anything but model sailors. But we really got into it: it wasn't all parties and drag races. I enjoyed looking after it and loved the whole culture of boat ownership. It was a great way to meet people, too.

The owners of many of the other boats in the marina were fairly wealthy and whenever you bumped into them you invariably talked to them about their boats, their families and what they did for a living. Because of that I made a lot of friends who have helped me over the years in business as well as football.

"Lots of those people, and indeed some of the players from my team, lived in the apartments that overlooked the marina. It was a tight-knit community and a bit like Neighbourhood Watch in a way. I'd get phone calls to say that kids were hovering around the boat at night; mostly they wanted their picture taken and I'd have to go down there, sign a few autographs and talk to them about football. It was a good thing, because once I did that they began to hang out at the marina and watch over the boats. It was great security.

"We kept the keys with the harbourmaster and if anyone wanted to take the boat out he'd let the others know in case they wanted to come along. One day I got a call from one of the other players who owned the boat with me. He lived by the marina and had a pair of binoculars that he used to watch everything that went on there. It seemed the boat was just a little too far away to determine who had taken it out.

"'Oh, it's not you who's taken the boat out, then,' he said as I answered the phone. 'It must be Jonesy.'

"I thought for minute. It was only 11am but although I hadn't fully come around I was with it enough to reply. 'Why didn't he tell us he was taking the boat out? It's beautiful outside; I'd probably have gone with him.'

"I could hear him fidgeting around with the binoculars, struggling for a better view of the boat. 'Well, I'm not entirely sure,' said my friend, 'but it could be because he's getting his end away with some blonde bird on the deck at the moment. Isn't his missus a brunette?'

"'That must be it,' I said. 'I'm going back to bed. Let me know when he's back.'

"Later that afternoon my friend phoned again: 'Jonesy's back. Fancy taking the boat out?' I did. It was a glorious day: the sun was beating down and although I couldn't see the sea from where I lived, I could just imagine it sparkling under a clear sky. I packed some towels, sunglasses, shorts and sun cream; I also put a change of clothes in as we'd decided to sail up the coast later that evening for a bite to eat in a restaurant that I'd booked.

"The three of us met down on the marina a little after 1pm. It was such a beautiful day that we decided to have lunch in one of the many restaurants that were dotted around. I remember that there was a great buzz in the air: it was the first really hot summer's day and people had naturally migrated down to the coast. We ordered our food and a bottle of Sauvignon Blanc. I'm a big Sauvignon Blanc fan, especially when the weather's good.

"The restaurant was busy and so was the area around it. We had perfect people-watching seats and as we started on our lunch I could feel the warmth of the wine wash over me. With it came the confidence to talk to the four women who had taken the table next to us.

69

"'Oh, you live there, do you?'

"'What do you do?'

"'What's your name?'

"'What do I do?'

"'It's that boat over there.'

"'Of course you can come.'

"That's how easy it is when you have a boat and the sun is shining, and before anybody could think of a reason not to, the four women had joined me, Jonesy and Tel on the boat and we were sailing out into the Channel.

"As soon as we were out the way of prying eyes, we turned the engine off and turned the music up. The coastguard had told us off before for loud music, but they weren't going to bother us out here. We weren't tempted to go for a dip. The sea was mucky and frothing inexplicably, and despite the heat of the sun the water was freezing. In any case, jumping into the sea from the side of a boat sounds like a fun thing to do but seems to yield very little pleasure when you actually do it. The ladies certainly seemed to share this opinion and remained dedicated to their day's work of sunbathing.

"As the afternoon wore on and the heat made way for the cooler air, we all made our way below deck to open the champagne that we'd brought with us. Some people say that four into three doesn't go, but I can tell you that, depending on what floats your boat, it does. The three of us headed off in different directions with a girl or two and a bottle of whatever was lying around. Somebody turned the music up in what seemed to me to be an attempt to drown out his own performance.

"I don't remember too much of what happened over the next couple of hours, but I do know that at some point I fell asleep, because I vividly recalled being startled awake by the sound of sirens coming from above deck. My first reaction was to panic because I had woken up disorientated, but then I realised it was the coastguard. The music was still going strong but there was no sign of the others.

"In the past I'd always been the one to deal with the coast-guard because I was fairly comfortable apologising on behalf of everyone. There are three things to remember where the coastguard are concerned: firstly, always acknowledge that you have done wrong with a grovelling apology – never make excuses. Secondly, always make sure the safety equipment on the boat is present and correct; otherwise, you simply give them a reason to hammer you. And lastly, never try to scramble around for that equipment while attempting to make your apology when drunk at sea with four near-naked women and two other footballers.

"As the coastguard stopped their engine and pulled alongside us, I could see that their faces did not have the usual 'We get this all the time' expressions. Instead, they looked pretty serious.

"'What are you doing out here?' shouted one of the officers.

"'Uh, nothing really,' I stammered. 'Just messing around.'

"That was a mistake: never say 'messing around' when you're at sea.

"'Follow us in to the mainland for a chat, please sir,' said the officer.

"This was worrying: we'd never had to go back for a chat before. Strange as it sounds, the first thing that came into my head was the paparazzi: they often snapped footballers down on the shore in the summer and they'd certainly love to get a shot of three players and four unknown women following the coastguard back for a 'chat'.

"In a panic I looked around for help. I needed something – anything – to avoid following the coastguard back in. And then I saw the shore. Immediately I relaxed: at worst, this was going to be a yellow card for persistent fouling. The coastguard had had enough of us and our loud music, I told myself, and was going to impose a fine. It was unfortunate but not the end of the world.

"I told the officer that I'd round up the people who were still below deck and that he could go on without us, as we weren't far from the shore. He'd be able to see me coming into the marina in a few minutes anyway. It wasn't as if I could speed away. 'Let me make sure that everyone knows we're about to leave first,' I said. 'I don't want them falling into things as I get up to speed. You go on and I'll follow.'

"'That's France, sir,' came the reply. 'Unless you want to drift back through the busiest shipping lanes in the world again, you should follow us.'

"'Yeah,' I said. 'We probably will, if that's all right.'

"On the way back we followed the coastguard closely but, as usually happens in these situations, it wasn't long before Jonesy became bored. As we were negotiating the shipping lanes, he decided that it might be more fun to follow a container ship that was passing ahead of us. He pulled the wheel hard to the left and in doing do scattered everybody on board to different parts of the boat. I was in the middle at the time and ended up shooting down the steps below deck.

"The pain was excruciating and I struggled for breath. It felt as if somebody was sticking a knife into me. I could hear the laughter from above but nobody came to check on me. I grabbed hold of a seat and managed to lever myself up before staggering back above deck. As soon as I reached the top step I saw Jonesy, who had been waiting for me. He was still at the wheel; before I could protest he shot it in the other direction and sent me careering toward the starboard side. I couldn't put my arms out in time and there was nothing to grab – I was heading over the side.

"Just as I took my last step and braced myself for a wet landing, an arm came out of nowhere and grabbed my hand. It was Tel. If he hadn't managed to stop me, I'd have gone over the edge and drowned for sure. I'm a decent swimmer but I could never have stayed afloat even for a second due to the injuries that I'd sustained moments before. I was still struggling to breathe and I couldn't move my arms from my sides.

"Thankfully the shore was coming into sight. The coastguard prevented any more boats from leaving the marina as we approached, and as we came in to moor I felt a huge sigh of relief wash over me.

"One of the officers came walking along the wooden walkway until he reached our boat as we were getting off. 'Jesus, what happened to you?' he said, looking at me.

'Nothing much,' I said. 'Just an old injury playing up, I think.' He didn't believe me but that wasn't why he was there and so he didn't press me on it. 'Listen lads,' he began, 'would you mind signing this for my boy?' And he produced a programme from the previous season.

"We looked at one another before fighting for the pen he was holding and signing as quickly as possible. Tel even gave the guy his phone number so he could bring his son down to a game when the new season started. We handed the programme back to him and as he turned to walk away he said, 'Just be careful on the boat, lads, OK? If you do go further out it might be an idea to drop anchor next time.'

"We stood by the boat before Tel said, 'Does that mean we can take the boat back out?'

"'Yes,' came the reply, 'but do me a favour and don't go near the shipping lanes. Luckily one of the container ships called us, otherwise who knows what could have happened?'

"'Come on, then,' said Tel. 'What time is that restaurant booked for?'

"'Seven,' I said, slinking back on to the boat.

"We made the short trip around the coast to a little private mooring that the restaurants and some of the homeowners occasionally used. There were no other boats as we tied up the Sunseeker and went inside to eat.

"The restaurant was packed and the wine was soon flowing. Some people came over to have their pictures taken with us; the mood in the place was laid back and happy. It's amazing what the sun can do for people. Everybody was having a great time; I'd even managed to forget that I still couldn't take a deep breath without wincing. The Sauvignon Blanc helped. After a couple of hours I forgot that I'd nearly been killed at sea that afternoon.

"Suddenly a huge crack reverberated around the restaurant, followed by a low groan. The noise had come from outside; two waiters were immediately dispatched to investigate. Thirty seconds later one of them came tearing back through the doors, shouting to the sommelier, who in turn briskly walked to the middle of the dining room and said, 'Ladies and gentleman, sorry for disturbing you, but may I ask which of you has tied a boat to the quay outside?'

"The whole restaurant turned to look in our direction and the sommelier walked toward us. 'Would you mind following me outside, sir?' he asked. 'There is a slight problem with the boat.'

"I followed him to the exit. The boat was a little way from the restaurant and couldn't be seen by the diners, but that didn't stop most of them from leaving their tables in our wake. I remember thinking that somebody had tried to steal it or, failing that, had vandalised it, but I couldn't think what they could have done that would have caused the noises that we had heard moments before.

"As we got nearer to where we had left the boat, I decided that it couldn't have been vandalised. It wasn't there any more – it must have been stolen. So why were we still walking towards the quay? Was the sommelier just trying to rub salt into the wound?

"'Sir,' he said, 'is this your boat?'

"I looked down. 'Er ... yes.'

"The boat hadn't been stolen after all. Instead it was hanging vertically from the quay by its stern, like a giant £1m plug hanging from a bath tap.

"All of us, diners included, stared at the yacht as it creaked from side to side.

"'What's happened?' said Tel.

"'What's happened?' I said, looking at him as if he were speaking a different language. 'What do you think's happened, Tel? The fucking tide's gone out, you dick.' I couldn't help remembering that he was the one who'd been so keen on sailing to the restaurant.

"The thing was, there wasn't anything that we could do. The boat would either fall, possibly to its death, in the next few minutes, or the tide would come back in and rescue it.

"'This is why nobody ever comes by boat,' said the sommelier.

"After what felt like the entire village had had their photographs taken with the boat, we returned to our table for dessert and waited for the tide to do its thing, which, eventually it did.

"'I could call the coastguard,' said the sommelier in the meantime.

"'No, don't do that! I mean, they're probably busy at sea.'

"When I finally managed to get to hospital I had two broken ribs and a collapsed lung. I missed the start of the next season. But at least I hadn't lost any teeth, unlike Tel."

THE PERKS OF THE TRADE

I've never had much interest in the perks that come with football. My golden years came about in part because I forfeited all the bullshit that came from success. I wanted to succeed in this game more than I wanted to revel in any of the spoils; believe me, there are plenty of players who choose to go about that in reverse. But I was also very lucky that I found a club that was a "project" or a "fixer-upper" in much the same way that, say, Leeds United or Sheffield Wednesday are – a big club that just needed a change in fortune. I decided that, on the pitch at least, I was going to be that change of fortune. I gave my body and my life for that football club: I helped them achieve things that they'd never achieved in their entire history. That club went on to enjoy their most successful period ever, sell out every week and, for a while at least, take on and beat almost everything that this country could offer. I made the owners hundreds of millions of pounds.

Now that I look back, I realise that I forfeited some amazing freebies – not that I could care less. In fact, in a weird way I feel pretty proud of myself for refusing to sell out.

You should have seen the look on the faces of boot suppliers when they'd turn up to the training ground to hand out vast amounts of crap, only for me to tell them I didn't want it. I think I get some kind of perverse pleasure out of it; it's the same pleasure I get from totally ignoring women who walk up next to me in a bar and start flinging their hair about. It isn't rudeness, although it probably comes across like that. I think it's more that I enjoy being in control of the situation.

But these opportunities never really go away, and depending on what it is a player is after, he can have pretty much anything he wants so long as he knows which number to call. I've turned down watches, sponsorship deals, golf club memberships, holidays, clothes, apartments (yes, really), phones ... the list goes on. One thing I did accept was a sponsored car because I refuse to buy cars. I cannot justify spending that amount of money on something that I know I won't get a return on. I also took tickets to see Kasabian at Earl's Court, though that almost ended badly after I got too close to Danny Dyer and had to dodge a hail of drinking vessels filled with piss.

Some perks simply have to be taken up for the greater good, however. I owe everything to my parents and I've tried to repay them as best I can over the years. I've taken them around the world, sent them to watch their heroes in concert and bought their house from them so they had no mortgage to pay (strictly speaking, that was to release equity to pay for my own ivory tower, but still ...). So when my father's team – and by extension my team – Tottenham drew AC Milan

THE PERKS OF THE TRADE

in the last 16 of the Champions League, I thought that this would be the perfect way to repay him. The problem was that the tickets were like the proverbial rocking horse shit. Worse, two of my friends – diehard Spurs fans – had decided to tag along, partly for the game but mainly because they smelled a good time brewing.

I tried everyone. I spoke to a couple of lads at Spurs but they had already given away their complimentary tickets, and I spoke to my own club, too – usually a last resort. Not many people know this, but every club gets a couple of tickets for any event held at Wembley on behalf of the FA; every year I put my name down for those tickets and at the end of every year I get offered silly money for them as somebody's team reaches an unexpected final. Liverpool have done very well for me over the years, in particular. Now, that has nothing to do with anything really, except that I had given tickets to the club secretary after her husband's team had got through to a final and I felt she owed me.

A very good trick for getting tickets is to go through your club secretary, who requests two tickets for "scouting purposes" for the club she represents. I have had great success with that in the past. Lo and behold, she contacted Milan and, as if by magic, they told her to piss off. They must know that one.

Just when all hope seemed lost, I was invited to lunch by one of my best mates and he asked me where I was watching the Tottenham game. There was only a week to go and so I told him that although I'd harboured ambitions of going to the San Siro, I'd probably left it too late now and so I'd end up watching it on the TV at home. I threw plenty of crocodile tears in because he tended to hang out with some pretty big-hitters. And it paid off. "Hold on a second, mate," he said. "Let me make a quick call." When he came back to the table, he was wearing one of those grins that said, "I can see how much it means to you, mate, and I'm glad to have been the friend who has sorted it for you. You'll owe me forever and that makes me happy." It was an amazing moment. "You need to call Paolo when you get there," he said. "He has the tickets and he'll take you in."

It transpired, rather bizarrely, that he'd rung Liam Gallagher, who at some point had been associated with Adidas, who sponsored AC Milan. It was a safe assumption that Adidas had a box at the San Siro as part of the deal, and that depending on who was asking there might be a couple of tickets kept aside for distant acquaintances of Adidas's "friends and family". And that, ladies and gentlemen, is the corporate equivalent of the six degrees of separation.

I rang my father: "You fancy going to the San Siro to watch the Tottenham match?" I rang my friends and told them the good news, and that I would get the flights for everyone just as soon as I was back home. True to form, by the time I arrived home they'd already booked the flights and, in an unexpected twist, had even booked one for me. It's amazing how happy football can make some people.

And so it was that, thanks to Liam Gallagher, my father and I and two friends met Paolo at the VIP entrance of the

San Siro in the middle of a monsoon and ascended those famous circular stairs until we reached the executive boxes. You get an impression of things from limited exposure, don't you – usually from TV, where it is easy to show something in a false glory. When I was a kid watching the Italia 90 World Cup, that stadium mesmerised me. It still does, but the reality is that when you walk up those stairs it's like wading up a waterfall of piss. My advice is to take the lift. Paolo led us to a door and said he'd leave us to it; we thanked him profusely and for once the kisses on both cheeks didn't feel awkward, even for my two friends, who simply don't kiss other men no matter what the circumstances. We had enjoyed an extended lunch and were still basking in the warm glow of a few bottles of a fantastic red wine, so we were happy to go along with anyone's traditions.

As I put my arm out to turn the handle, the door opened to reveal a stunning and very smiley Italian woman whose name I've forgotten but whose phone number I still have, saved under "Stunning Italian woman". Let's call her Isabelle, if only because I like that name. She welcomed us in and showed us around what was without doubt the finest executive box I have ever seen. On the right-hand side, down the entire length of the wall, was a shrine to Adidas that encompassed pictures of, among others, David Beckham, wearing the red-and-black stripes of Milan, with a pair of his white Predator boots – signed, of course – in a glass case. There were memorabilia from a host of legendary players – shirts, boots, trophies and so on, all signed and proudly displayed.

I've seen a lot of this sort of thing and it usually comes across as garish, but now I couldn't help but be impressed. Perhaps it was because of the quality of the players.

Underneath were fridges of beers and Cokes, and there was a huge plasma screen where you could watch replays of the game if you missed something live. Along the back wall was a bar with an impressive array of drinks and a young man eager to pour them, and in the middle of the room was an enormous table groaning under the weight of incredible-looking food including hand-carved hams, olives the size of plums and pasta dish upon pasta dish, each more inviting than the last. At one end of the table a waiter stood ready to dispense plates, glasses and cutlery. I've been in executive boxes all over the world and for the most part they are like hotel rooms – if you've seen one, then you've definitely seen them all. But this was the real deal. I remember thinking that if I ever had anything to do with a football club's corporate entertainment, then this would be the level to aspire to – the basic things such as food, comfort, a bit of memorabilia and service but done really, really well.

"And out of these doors you can see the pitch and your seats, please gentlemen," said Isabelle. "Please, you only let me know what you want and I will make it happen for you." I bit my tongue, mainly because double entendres remind me of shit Carry On films, but also because the view left you speechless. The box was smack bang on the halfway line, just below the level of the camera angle that you see on the TV. You have to hand it to the Italians: they know how to do things with style, and out of the 80,000 people who would be packed in to the San Siro that night there was no doubt who had the best seats. As I wandered outside, the full scale of the San Siro hit me and I silently repeated what a friend once said to me when I took him on a tour of the stadium at my first big club: "Ahhh, proper football."

There was still an hour to kick-off, so we made the most of the hospitality. The waiter took the cork out of a very good Barolo and poured in earnest, and we sat around like kings of the San Siro until the team sheet arrived. The first name we all looked for was Gareth Bale, who'd destroyed Inter Milan over two legs earlier in the season and was looking like the real deal. But he wasn't there. That was unfortunate because earlier I'd taken a call from a friend of mine at the Guardian who had told me that Bale was fit and was going to start. Although he'd warned me against telling anyone until it was confirmed, I couldn't resist and tweeted something like, "A little bird tells me that Gareth Bale is fit and starts in the San Siro." I later tweeted that I'd shot that particular bird.

The stadium began to fill up; the Tottenham fans were way up in the heavens and although we could hear them we couldn't see them due to the thick, foggy blanket above us and the smoke from the flares. I phoned a mate who was up in the rafters among the Tottenham fans – he's a season ticket holder, before you ask why he wasn't invited with us – and he said that none of them could see the pitch yet. Isabelle told us that kick-off was imminent and escorted us to our seats, from where we could see that, apart from being the only four people in the box not in an immaculate made-to-measure suit with sunglasses, we were also the only Englishmen.

As the game started the noise levels were incredible. Somebody let off one of those bangers that sound loud even when you hear them on TV, and it was greeted with what was probably the loudest cheer of the night as far as the Milan fans were concerned. When the first half came to an end, amazingly Tottenham had held their own, although in truth Milan had offered almost nothing. Seedorf was having an off night and was being jeered by a section of the Milan fans as a result, and Ibrahimovic looked as if he'd forgotten that there was a game tonight, had made other plans for the evening and was now sulking after having to reschedule. Even so, Michael Dawson was still having the game of his life against the big Swede.

At half time we made our way back through the doors and into the warmth of the box, where I helped myself to some more Barolo. Just then the door opened and an impossibly sharp-looking Italian man walked in, followed by a second man who entered with the aid of a pair of crutches. I recognised the first as Gianluca Zambrotta and the second as Filippo Inzaghi. If we were in the UK, even in the Premier League, they'd have both been in horrible club tracksuits but this was Italy and AC Milan, so they were dressed impeccably in their own clothes. Inzaghi had a beautiful leather jacket that, as my friend commented, "probably cost more than my car". True, but then so would a shit leather jacket.

I don't think I've ever been star-struck and this was no exception, but they are legends of the game and I found myself walking towards them and shaking their hands just so I could tell them so. Unfortunately my friend wasn't able to style it out quite so coolly and proceeded to tell Inzaghi that he used to buy him regularly on Championship Manager when he was a Juventus player.

At that point I decided to grab a plate of food and another glass of wine. I made sure that I sat down directly in front of the table, so that I was in easy reach of the bottle I'd been enjoying and had every intention of finishing. My father still hadn't come in from his seat and was busy taking pictures of everything and soaking up the atmosphere. Just then Isabelle received a call on her radio and stiffened as if royalty were expected at any moment. There was a quick spruce-up of the box and readjusting of clothing and hair before she stood by the door, waited for the shadow of a figure to loom over the frosted glass and turned the handle just before the person on the other side would have to do it himself. In walked Fabio Capello.

I had a friend who played in the Premier League for many years and earned a fortune; whenever I'd ask how he was doing he'd say, "Very wealthy, thank you." For some reason, the moment I asked Capello how he was, that reply popped into my head. Not for the first time he let me down. "Very well, thank you. How are you?"

"Pretty good," I said. "How did you get in here?"

"Ah, good," came the reply, coupled with a half-smile. I slunk back into my seat and poured another glass of Barolo while Capello sidled up to the table.

The reason it was uncomfortable for both of us is that a few years earlier, when Capello had taken the England job, he had held a press conference in which he'd made it clear that it was time for the England squad to grow up. Misbehaviour would no longer be tolerated. A day later I received a call from a journalist friend who said he had it from two good sources at the FA that I was in Capello's England squad. I think it was some of the guys who arrange transport for the players.

Not for the first time, I celebrated too early and far, far too well. This time, it proved to be a monumental, career-defining mistake. The next morning my name was every-where – newspapers, TV, the internet – everywhere, except on the list of Fabio Capello's England squad. Until this point my career had been going up and up and up, and it isn't an exaggeration to say that at that exact moment my love for football, my desire to play and, ultimately, my career fell off a cliff. Still, it makes for a great story.

I like to think that our meeting was an awkward one for Capello because it reminded him that he was not a man of his word. He made it crystal clear in that same press confer-ence that it didn't matter which player committed an offence – the result would always be the same. We now know that, depending on the player in question, that was bullshit.

The box had filled up a little bit, to the point that there were now a dozen people or more milling around. Just then, my father and my friend walked in, rubbing their hands together and pointing out that it was still cold outside.

"Nil-nil," said my friend. "We're in danger of doing something here." He came around the table to sit next to me, and my father walked up to the table for a quick heart-starter. Neither of them had noticed Capello, and I waited for them to realise who was in the room with them. But they didn't.

In Milan, at least, it is tough to find anyone held in greater esteem than Fabio Capello. Some of the memorabilia we were sitting near harked back to his great Milan sides of the early 90s. He won four Serie A titles, three Coppa Italias, a European Cup and a European Super Cup during his time with the Rossoneri. But now he was just a man looking for a drink.

I sat there looking straight at my father and Fabio Capello standing next to each other, each deciding what they were going to plump for. I was no more than six feet away from it all and my smile was getting wider. Just then Capello leaned across my father to reach for a glass at the other end of the table – and probably wished he hadn't. "Oi, fuck off, John! What's your game?" said my father. "If you want a glass, just ask for one. Don't lean across people." The best thing was that at no point did he notice that this was Fabio Capello because he never once looked up. I sat there in a state of semi-paralysis watching the episode unfold; I hadn't managed to get the olive that I was holding into my mouth and my eyes were on stalks.

My father reached for a glass and passed it to Capello, who thanked him before filling it and wandering off. My father came to sit down next to me. "Bloody people," he said.

I stared straight ahead for a moment trying to think of the right words.

"Dad," I said. "I think you just told Fabio Capello to fuck off."

"Eh?"'

"I said, I think you just told Fabio Capello to fuck off."

• • •

As the teams came out for the second half, my father and one of my friends took their seats. My other friend and I stayed inside and watched on the TV, mainly because it was bloody freezing and the Barolo was going down far too easily. Capello had disappeared and it wasn't long before the two Milan players had seen enough. Inzaghi raised a hand and said, "I see you." I wasn't sure if he was saying goodbye or simply commenting on the fact that we were extremely conspicuous in our surroundings, but as he limped toward the door I took it to be the former and bade him a friendly "Ciao, Pippo." To this day, he remains the coolest man I've ever met.

The game was drifting towards a memorable draw, a result that none of my Tottenham-supporting friends had thought even remotely possible. I stood to top up my glass just as the ball fell to Luka Modrić. It's a strange thing about football: if you play this game long enough with a certain level of intensity, you are sometimes able to spot promising situations way before they happen, just by the way the players are positioned and which players are on the ball – sometimes even before the ball has reached the player who can set the move off. You get a gut feeling that something is about to happen, your brain puts everything together in a nanosecond and you realise: "Modrić is a great passer who sees things very quickly; if he can slip that ball in to Lennon then nobody will catch Lennon; if he can draw one of those defenders out, neither of whom are quick, and get past him, then Tottenham have a great chance to score because Milan are all over the place."

It reminds me of Ronnie O'Sullivan coming to the snooker table for his shot and knowing that he is about to make a 147 even before the first ball is potted, just from the way the first red is positioned.

When Modrić pushed the ball through to Lennon I made a break for the door, pausing only to glug the remaining Barolo. As Lennon ran with the ball the pattern of play was working out just as my brain had told me it would: Milan were hopelessly exposed and the fastest player on the pitch had the ball with metres of clear grass to run it to. I was halfway down the executive box and had jettisoned the wine glass. The door was shut and needed to be opened, using up precious seconds; as I got closer to the window I could see Lennon sprinting down the far side of the pitch and the Milan defender, Mario Yepes, holding his ground. I lunged for the door just as Yepes lunged at Lennon, but he had no chance. I already knew Lennon was going to get past him rather than take the foul because he would have seen Peter Crouch in his peripheral vision sprinting into the box alongside him.

I opened the door just as Lennon entered the box. My father and my friend began to get out of their seats as they saw Crouch arriving too. Lennon squared the ball perfectly and, with one long sweep of his right leg, Crouch turned the ball past Christian Abbiati at the exact moment that I bundled into the back of my friend and my father. We went absolutely nuts and in doing so drew the attention of about 500 or so sharply dressed Italian men who had turned around to see who was responsible for the noise in what was usually the safest Milan seat in the house.

Now, I know that all sounds like a cheap imitation of the film Fever Pitch at the moment when Michael Thomas scores the winner for Arsenal against Liverpool at Anfield in the 1989 championship decider – but, hand on heart, that is exactly what happened.

The last 10 minutes were tense, but unbelievably Tottenham held on. When the final whistle sounded there was an almighty roar to our left from somewhere way up in the heavens. My father and I hugged each other and in a sudden release of pent-up emotion we began to cry. Neither of us ever thought that we'd see Tottenham beat AC Milan in the Champions League at the San Siro – it was a hugely emotional moment for both of us. Football is more than a game to my father. He once refused to watch me play again after my debut for a Premier League club because he didn't believe that they were playing football the way it should be played. He said to me, "I didn't drive you around for all those years as a kid to have to watch you play football like that."

He was absolutely right. I told my new manager that I wanted to leave his football club the next day, six weeks after I'd signed. That's what football means to me ... to us.

We walked around the executive box in a daze for a few minutes, trying to work out where we were going to carry on the party. Isabelle came back into the room and I grabbed her in a weak attempt to show what a good mover I was, even though it's obvious to everyone that I have two left feet. "Where are we going, Isabelle?" I asked. She laughed and made some poor excuse about having to stay in the box and make sure it was tidied, so I told her that if she didn't come with me of her own free will I was going to take her with me anyway. She gave me one of those looks somewhere between mock surprise and genuine intrigue before grabbing a beautiful leather jacket, slipping it over her made-to-measure black uniform and pulling me toward the door. We waited for a taxi outside some apartment blocks next to the San Siro and bumped into the Milan full-back Ignazio Abate, who had driven back from the ground to an apartment that he had in this block. I told him we were looking for a cab – that was the Barolo talking – and he said to ask the concierge and pointed me towards a guy behind a little window to one side of the main gate. Nice guy, considering he'd just lost at home in the Champions League to Tottenham.

Isabelle told the driver to take us to a hotel and I assumed it must have a decent bar with a good crowd. When we arrived it was an enormous five-star effort that exuded Italian opulence. As we walked in security was tight and we eventually found our way to a roped-off entrance flanked by two security guards. "Here is your friends," said Isabelle; I looked inside and there were the Spurs team celebrating. Almost immediately I became extremely uncomfortable. There's an unwritten rule in football: no matter how well you know other teams' players, no matter how much they say, "Come out with us," you never, ever, muscle in on their celebrations. It looks desperate and clingy. Still, I made sure I had a good look around first.

We still managed to celebrate in style, drinking well into the small hours with a group of Spurs season ticket holders before heading back to my hotel for a nightcap. It, too, was heaving with fans clinging on to the memory of a famous night in the San Siro. I slipped into bed and reflected for a moment on an unbelievable day.

I spoke to Isabelle first thing the next morning and over coffee she told me that she slept very comfortably. So that was nice.

PART TWO
WHERE NOW?

Where else could I play?
What else could I do?

BANG GOES PLAN A

It used to be the case that once a player was older and had proved himself, possibly won a couple of things and earned some standing in the game, he could move closer to home and have his pick of the smaller local clubs. Whoever signed him could expect to sell a few more tickets and a few more shirts, as well as having an experienced older professional to help with the younger players. It was a good deal for everyone and it allowed the older players to grab a couple of extra years on the pitch while they waited for their pension to mature, got a foot on the coaching ladder or even tried their hand at management.

But that cosy arrangement is changing, thanks to legislation passed down from Uefa, the long and short of which is that no club will be allowed to spend more than 60 per cent of its turnover on wages. It is widely expected that these rules will reach Europe's top leagues within two years; they are already in place in the lower divisions, where some clubs have been hit with transfer embargoes for breaching them. This has led to an interesting situation for clubs and players alike: those players who can be used in several positions are being retained and joined by others who are young, hungry and, above all, cheap. But for those players looking to nab an extra year or two before they retire, things are tougher. Squad sizes are being cut and the options to play are limited.

This has hit a few of my friends hard. I have never known so many players out of a job – good players, too. Players who are extremely capable and dependable can't even get a foot in the door. I called a mate who had always harboured ambitions of playing for MK Dons because he lives in Milton Keynes; he's had a good career, much of it spent in the Premier League, and isn't too worried about the wages on offer. He told me that MK Dons' failure to win promotion to the Championship has led to a change in policy at the club and they are now only signing players who are 25 or under.

Now, that could just be something that they told him so he'd sod off but, worryingly for the older players, this policy actually works. When Yeovil won promotion from League One last season, they did it on a total wage budget of £800,000 a year. This season that will rise to £2m, but to put that figure into context it is still £3.2m a year less than Christopher Samba's annual wage when he was at QPR, a team Yeovil will now be playing in the Championship.

Uefa seems to have given little thought to the players affected by its cost protocol. We're not talking about players who have enjoyed success at the highest level; we're talking about the players who have been at Rochdale their entire career, with two kids, earning £600 a week with a

£1,000-a-month mortgage. There are a huge number of these players and, in my opinion, Uefa and Platini have completely shafted them.

The positions of many other members of staff are also being cut because the wages cap doesn't only cover players, so those clubs that looked to do things professionally by employing chefs, sports scientists and masseurs are now finding that they are having to let them go, no matter how heavily subsidised those positions were by private money.

All of which makes for an uncertain future for footballers like me, who are finding out that there is indeed a wrong side of 30. And that has led to some "out of the box" thinking. Many of my friends have now moved to Australia, North America, Indonesia, the UAE and all over Europe to improve their prospects, and it's striking how many say the same thing: "Come out here to play – you'd love it." Now, either they're liars and like the idea of bringing somebody else down with them, or there is actually something to be said for playing football abroad.

I have always liked the idea; I have played with many fantastic foreign players who have made their money in this country and returned home to play, in much the same way that English players want to play for their local club when they are coming to the end of their careers.

When your back is against the wall, you either crumble or you come out fighting. I went for the latter, aided admirably by the drugs I now take, pulled out my Rolodex and began calling people. And do you know what I found? I actually know a lot of people.

So towards the end of last season I began to put some feelers out through my agent, while at the same time talking with a few acquaintances at some of these distant clubs. Inexplicably, that's something I failed to do in the past, much to my cost. When I made my big career move, I neglected to check what the town was like, what the people were like, the manager, the facilities, the ambitions, the style of football, the expectations – nothing. It was crazy on my part because there were an awful lot of people I could have asked, but the club flashed up pound signs and reeled me in. I vowed never to make the same mistake again.

WHAT ABOUT RUSSIA?

I have to be honest: Russia has never appealed to me as either a country to visit or as a place to ply my trade. It's probably a lovely place but for a huge area it's noticeable how rarely it features in any 1,000 Places To See Before You Die guides. But at the risk of talking about something that I know very little about, that is probably due to its political history, its perception of the outside world and ours of it. It is more than likely a very misunderstood place that few casual observers have the inclination to try to understand anyway. So when I took a phone call last summer – from an American agent, ironically – it was hard to know how to react: would playing in Russia be a good thing or not? I didn't have the faintest.

Most of what we hear about Russia these days is to do with its considerable wealth, which stems mainly from its huge natural resources. "Oligarch" is now a word that everyone is familiar with. But it is obvious to most of us that people rarely become that rich without taking care of the right officials along the way, and those who fall out with the Kremlin seem to either end up in jail or go missing in action.

So playing football in Russia isn't exactly an opportunity that I'd go running towards with my arms wide open, because if it can happen to the richest in the land, then it can happen to anybody.

There is a well-known story in football circles about a British player who left the UK to play for one of the big Moscow clubs. His wages were rumoured to be around £20,000 a week, which was fantastic given his age and what he'd achieved in his career. I remember hearing the story from one of his new team-mates that I bumped into in Dubai. The player in question had told him that he'd once been sitting in the changing rooms at half time, 2-0 down during a big local derby match. Suddenly, the door swung open and in walked the owner – it's not uncommon for that to happen. He spoke in Russian for less than a minute before walking out again. One of his team-mates told him through a combination of sign language and cracked English that the owner had just offered every player a £50,000 bonus if they pulled off a win – and, amazingly, they did. They won the game 3-2 and this player actually managed to score. The first day back at the training ground after the game a man turned up, presumably sent by the chairman, with £50,000 in cash for everyone who played in the game. The scorers got £25,000 each on top.

There's nothing wrong with cash payments, of course, so long as the proper declarations are made, but let's not kid ourselves that was going to happen here. The biggest problem was getting it back into the country: the player was advised to buy a car and then use the leftover cash to import it to the UK, as soon as possible.

This practice isn't unique to Russia, by the way. There is a chairman in the Championship who pays almost exclusively in cash. You've probably seen the pictures on Instagram and Facebook, or even in the papers, of players who have received a big pile of cash and have decided to pose with it placed over their crotch, for example. They make out that it's cash they've just drawn out of the bank, but that money has been paid by the owner as a signing-on fee or a loyalty bonus. After all, it doesn't say in your contract that every payment has to be made by bank transfer, even if that's the way that most of working society operates today. The owner does the same when paying off contracts early. I remember a player moving from this club and a man in a beautiful Mercedes turning up at the hotel with a suitcase full of cash – literally a suitcase.

The thing is, if an owner in Russia is promising sums like the ones I've just mentioned on a whim at halftime, the chances are that he's bet an awful lot of money on the game, perhaps with the other team's owner. As my friend and I sat around that pool in Dubai, the idea of huge piles of cash arriving out of thin air appealed to us until he pointed out that for every winner there is a loser. For all those matches when you receive a cash bonus for winning, there are others that you will lose – and when you lose the owner a lot of money, that puts your own wages at risk. On more than one occasion this player wasn't paid, and what could he do about it? He took the money in the bag when he won, so he was over a barrel when he lost. He couldn't say, "It's not fair," not in Russia. But it sounded as if it evened out in the end; in fact, I'm told that you'd have to be doing very badly indeed not to be considerably up on your basic contract by the end of the season.

I can just about get my head around that. I'm not a prude about such things and I understand how certain businesses work. And on the plus side, there are a lot of quality players in Russia now and the clubs there are improving year on year. In fact, those who know about these things are tipping Russia's clubs to make the biggest impact on European football in the next 10 years. A good friend of mine who knows Aiden McGeady told me that when he left Celtic for Spartak Moscow in 2010 he had every intention of staying for a year before returning to Britain to join a Premier League team. He's still out there.

But some things I just can't ignore. I played with a black player from Africa, a nice fella though absolutely crazy. He had come to us from a big Russian club and the stories he told were horrendous. He had skinheads waiting for him outside the training ground most days – and these were "fans" of the club. Sometimes they caught him and he'd get a pasting; other times he'd get away in a pre-booked cab. That isn't a place where I want to play football. I have many black friends and I don't want to be around that.

WHAT ABOUT CHINA?

Damiano Tommasi, the former Roma player, is now an agent who works a lot in the Chinese market; there aren't many deals for European players heading out to China where he's not involved. I have to admit that I thought it would be easy to join them. It's China, right? I'm British, played in the Premier League, pretty good reputation and still young enough: they love all that, don't they?

I phoned my agent, who is more than used to my spur-of-the-moment madness. He's earned a small fortune out of me down the years, but also had to put up with a hell of a lot.

"Look, take this in the way that it is meant," he said, "but you struggled to live 200 miles away from where you grew up. How are you going to get on 10,000 miles away? I know there were 'circumstances' around that" – depression talk makes him uncomfortable – "but still. You don't speak the language and you don't know anything about the place. I have to be honest, mate: it's not something I can recommend. Look, you've known me long enough now. It's not about my payday – if you said to me, 'I've considered all that but I really want you to look at it,' then you know that I would. But I'm talking to you as a friend now" – he always says that when he's stressing a point that he feels is important – "I don't think it's the right move for you. You've got young children to think of and it isn't just you any more doing what you want to do."

He is very persuasive; something that I'd told myself not to fall for long before I picked the phone up. The trouble is that the longer the conversation went on, the more I wondered if my stubbornness was getting in the way of the right decision. They're very good, these agents.

In the end, I made a token effort to assert my position as a man who is in control of his life. "I hear what you're saying, mate," I said, "and as ever I appreciate your input but I really feel that I'd like you to make some calls and at least find out what the situation is over there. I already know that in all likelihood I'm probably not going to China but it never hurts to have a couple of backup plans."

So he made a call to Tommasi and got a very clear answer. "Look," Tommasi told him. "Really the clubs are looking for European players who are between 25 and 28. They'll bend the rules for truly world-class players who can be used to attract names like Drogba and Anelka but, with all due respect, your player isn't at that level and he isn't between those ages any more."

"There really isn't anything out there?"

"I'll give you an idea of how tough it is," said Tommasi. "China has already turned down Inzaghi and Luca Toni. That's what you're up against."

I know when I'm beaten.

WHAT ABOUT SCOTLAND?

"A'reet bawbag?"

"Hello, mate," I said. "How's things?"

"Aye, no bad pal. I'm un Bob Marley's hem in Jamaica and a family has just wucked in, all wearing ma shirt wi' ma name on the back. Fuckin' chances, pal? Tiny little house, two hours from the hotel and a got a tap on the shoulder and there's a family of five asking me for a photo."

"Mate, it's because you're Scotland's biggest export these days," I laughed.

"You'se a fucking pruck. What d'ya want, like?"

"I've got an offer to go to Scotland and wanted your opinion."

"Oh Jeezuz, mate," he said. "Is thut what ut's come too? Nay bother, pal, fire away."

I don't mean to cause offence, though I probably already have, but in recent years Scotland has become a destination for English clubs to send players on loan who aren't good enough to play in the Premier League, in the hope that they'll score a few goals in an easier league before some naive manager back in England takes a punt. It's happened time and again; I'm sure you can all think of a player who went from Arsenal to Scotland to Sunderland, and the manager who took the bait back in England. What makes Scotland perfect for this is its proximity and the fact that for the size of its league system it has two enormous clubs that are well known around Europe, possibly even the world. Certainly Rangers are well known in Gran Canaria, where as a young man I was kicked out of the Barry Ferguson Loyal bar. You have to be pretty badly behaved to get kicked out of a Scottish football supporters' pub. There were no such problems at Linekers around the corner. Happy to have you, are Gary and his brother; just don't dance on their bar – it's frowned upon.

The offer I had was from one of the two giants of Scottish football and came because I knew the coach there at the time. I was completely sold on the idea, actually. A chance to play for a huge team in the Champions League!

I already had a view on playing in Scotland, and it was the same view as probably 99 per cent of Premier League players who look north of the border. It would be easier, it would be a chance to show off, to look better than everything around me and to win something – a league, a cup, medals – because that's what it's about, after all. So I rang this friend who used to play for Celtic for what I thought would be the final endorsement. I'm dropping the Scottish accent now because it's painful to type like that.

"It's hard mate, really hard. Don't go unless you're in good nick, seriously, or you want to get your head down and work hard. It's not a jolly, pal: these people up here aren't grateful that you're coming to play for them – it's the other way around. It's a way of life for them, and it doesn't matter if you're the greatest player in the world – if you have a bad game you are going to know about it, and not on Monday morning but 20 minutes into the game. If the team aren't a goal up inside 20 minutes the boos will start, and if you're a goal down it becomes a really tough atmosphere to play in. Even if you grind it out 2-1 the papers will be full of blood come Monday morning. There's pressure everywhere, pal. You'll not escape it. Doesn't matter if you're playing in an Old Firm game or against Raith Rovers in the Scottish Cup – everyone wants to beat you. I've seen some incredibly talented players crumble and leave the club after six months or a year because they just couldn't cope with it every week."

"What about the home fans?" I asked.

There was silence for a couple of seconds. "I'm talking about the home fans, ya fuckin' twat!

"The away fans are even worse. When I played for one of the big-hitters it was hatred, pal, and I do mean hatred. You've never experienced anything like it until you've played for one of them. I'd pull up to traffic lights in my car and I'd get one of three things: a thumbs-up, a middle finger or a fight ... and that was anywhere that you went in the city. There were no safe havens – everyone was everywhere all of the time. You'll be thinking, 'Shall we go to dinner here tonight?' and then you realise, 'No, we can't, because it's a religious day or the owner of the place supports one or the other team.' It's constant, 24/7: every time you have a beer, every time you buy a paper, every time you leave the house, every person you meet, it's Rangers, Celtic, Rangers, Celtic."

"Yeah, but it must be nice to win things," I said.

"Aye, of course, pal, but that doesn't just happen. You don't just win because you play for one of the big two – the effort that goes in is twice that of any other team. What people don't realise is that as an Old Firm player you'd come back from a huge Champions League game late Tuesday or Wednesday night, a game in which generally you'd be chasing shadows for 90 minutes but because of sheer commitment, energy and the demands of the fans you'd get a positive result. Then you'd have Thursday off and travel to Dundee or Edinburgh on Friday to play against 11 players who are so fired up to beat you it's a joke. It's their biggest game of the season, the stadium is sold out, it's on TV, and you're completely fucked: you're so tense, you're begging for somebody just to bag a quick double to take the effort out of the game. It is draining to come back from playing a huge European team and see that you're playing Motherwell at home on a Saturday at 3pm. Honestly, it's so mentally tough and it's tough on the body, too."

"So what are the Old Firm games like to play in?" I asked. There was a long, drawn-out breath at the end of the phone.

"It isn't just the game, pal. The build-up to an Old Firm match starts weeks earlier. The press have got it every day for weeks: interviews, pictures, past games, predictions … It's relentless.

"I was surprised when I played in them. Everybody told me that the games were just a case of smash and grab – I'd need to be fit and go around smashing people – but there was so much more to them. They were so quick. You'd get found out very quickly in an Old Firm game: I've seen good players play in one and never in another, and I've seen talented players unable to handle the occasion altogether. I did well in most of them, we had a decent record, and because of that the away fans hated me even more. You know what it's like: if any player does well in their career they get abused by rival fans. I scored in an Old Firm game once and the fucking hate mail I got the next week was insane. I opened one letter and reached in to pull out what I thought was a letter; when I held it up it was a piece of toilet tissue that somebody had wiped their arse on.

"For about a week after the game my phone was ringing non-stop – every hour of the day – and it was always the same: people singing sectarian songs. You start getting paranoid, looking out the window at cars driving past and people standing in the street. It was fucking scary. I was just about to get a new number and then, exactly a week after it had started, it stopped."

"What's the standard like, though?" I asked. "Would I go mad in frustration?"

"It is what it is, pal. Scotland gets a bad name because of the standard outside the Old Firm, or Celtic now, but remember Celtic are competing in the last 16 of the Champions League off the back of £2m in TV money, and what do your

Sunderlands and your Stokes get? £65m? £70m? That's pretty special if you ask me, and before long Rangers will be back up there and it'll all start again. If you win something, well, you win something. You can only beat what's in front of you, can't you? And try telling the fans up there that it's not as important as the Premier League. If you want to go, you should go, but if you've got any doubts you should go somewhere else because it will take over your life."

"OK, mate," I said. "I'll let you go. I can't listen to Buffalo Soldier in the background any more."

"Nay bother, pal. I'm away to the wee bar at the hotel anyway for the gallon [eight pints], so I'll speak to ya in a bit. A'reet, bawbag?"

I don't think Scotland is for me.

WHAT ABOUT
THE MIDDLE EAST?

I'll be honest: I didn't have any offers to play from the Middle East, but then again, I wasn't really looking. If I'd had a decision to make, then I could well have been tempted. But having nothing on the table in terms of playing doesn't mean that there aren't opportunities for an ageing footballer who fancies working in that part of the world. Abu Dhabi Media, which owns the TV rights to the Premier League in 27 countries across the Middle East, flies out current and former Premier League players to summarise the matches live in its studios, much in the same way that if Liverpool were playing Manchester City on live TV, Sky might draft in Craig Bellamy or Robbie Fowler for relevance and possibly some insider knowledge.

Fees for this kind of punditry in Abu Dhabi start at around £10,000 for a player of my level – extremely nice work considering they fly you out, put you up in a luxury hotel and feed and water you over a long weekend. That makes it a little easier to work out why Rio Ferdinand turned down last season's England call-up and flew to Abu Dhabi instead. If a player of my standard can command a basic fee of £10,000, first-class flights and access to a well stocked minibar, imagine what the big-hitters are demanding. £100,000? Even for half of that, it's a nice weekend's work. It is certainly not beyond the realm of possibility: Alan Hansen was on £40,000 a show as a pundit for Match of the Day, if his leaked contract is to be believed.

Unfortunately, in my case it's The Secret Footballer who has the reputation for punditry, not the man behind the pseudonym, so I'm stuck between a rock and a hard place. As TSF, I have been able to write columns for Abu Dhabi TV, but as far as appearing on screen there is concerned, the closest I've come is steering some fellow players in that direction. I suppose that's a fundamental flaw in the anonymous model: some areas simply can't be exploited.

What about other business opportunities? A friend of mine is a venture capitalist for technology companies: he graduated from Harvard with a business master's and has raised about £200m for startups down the years. He is seriously switched on and genuine with it. Last season we were having lunch at our favourite restaurant when he told me that he'd recently had a meeting with a Qatari fund that was looking to invest in a football club. "They're great people," he said, "and they love the English heritage. They were very keen on Nottingham Forest because of the history but they lost out, so why don't we find a club, do the deal and install you as chairman, like Niall Quinn at Sunderland?"

It was a good idea but certainly not that simple. Still, he had my attention.

"I've had several meetings with these guys now and they are adamant that they will be buying a club in the next two years," he said. "So why don't you do some research and find out through your contacts which clubs are for sale as a start? Then we'll form a partnership and become the broker for the deal."

This is a similar approach to that taken by Adam Pearson, who left his position at Leeds in the Premier League to purchase Hull City, who were then in the bottom tier of English football and in administration. He got them into the Championship before selling out and buying a majority stake in Derby County and trying again. Derby are a huge club that would easily fill their stadium if they were to get back to the Premier League.

I started to make some calls, and do you know what I found? There are a lot of football clubs for sale.

My first call was to the owner of a big Midlands club that have been down on their luck for some time. They pull in huge crowds, have planning permission to take their capacity close to 50,000 and offer first-class training facilities. There's a huge amount of work that goes into these deals but the starting point is always a friendly call followed by lunch. During that lunch the owner told me that he had other interests that he wanted to pursue and that maybe it was time for someone new to come in, throw some money at the club and see what happened. "What would you want for it?" I asked.

He didn't hesitate, "Lock, stock and barrel, I'd take £40m," he said. For a broker whose business would net between 10 and 20 per cent of any deal, that's a hell of a payday.

The work involved would be considerable, of course: there are EBITDAs to pore over (something that gives the true picture of a company's value and profitability) and the potential to factor in. But that would be handled by experts. Although I understand and enjoy business, in this instance I would be the "football face" of any deal, telling investors why the club I was recommending was such a fantastic opportunity, while sprinkling in stories from the pitch and changing room.

So far we have identified three clubs; the owners of two are keen to sell, while the third's would prefer to remain involved with the club, subject to any investment. Two are in the Championship and the other is in League One. The value of most football clubs lies in their potential, helped in no small part by the wealth of the party looking to take them over. At first I looked for clubs that had no debt – not easy – but I soon realised that debt is not the overriding concern for many wealthy investors. When Pearson went into Derby, the club had debts rumoured to be in excess of £25m but he still had backing from an American consortium. The fact is that when you're dealing with an extremely rich investment fund, as we are, £25m of debt is neither here nor there. The decision is primarily about the history and pedigree of the club, and its potential.

Debt is really only a factor for consortia that are looking for a healthy stake in a club rather than an outright takeover.

Most debt can be wiped out within a single year in the Premier League, although getting to the promised land is becoming tougher, and not just because of the strong competition in the Championship and beyond. Even if Bill Gates and all his billions wanted to buy a football club there are now other factors to consider. Recently the Uefa fair play model has seen a succession of clubs, mainly in Leagues One and Two, hit with transfer embargoes. The last club I heard of that was spending more than 60 per cent of their turnover was Swindon. (But if we're talking about spending, whenever Swindon have an injury, they send the player to Rome for treatment.)

* * *

I have another link to the Middle East, now I think about it. Years ago, I went on a tour to Ras al-Khaimah. God knows why, given that nobody in our squad had even heard of it – it must have been a bent deal with some official at our club and some wealthy people in that part of the world. We landed in Dubai and drove along the coast to "the RAK", which is about an hour north of its wealthier cousin. After a long day we arrived at our hotel on the beachfront and it was like a little bit of paradise. I'd never seen anything like it, yet I immediately felt at home. The development was brand new and the people extremely welcoming. After a few days of tough training in which our manager came up with his usual ridiculous ideas like sprinting along the beach and kicking up sand in the faces of the holidaymakers, before swimming out to sea, around the buoy and back again – something that saw a few of the African lads nearly drown – I was exhausted.

Fortunately, the coaches recognised this and persuaded the manager to give us a day off. It helped that our game had been called off. I think we were supposed to play a Bahrain XI – nothing dodgy about that, then.

On the day off the lads decided to take a bus back to Dubai to go shopping in the malls, something that appealed to me about as much as a bout of malaria. So instead I took a stroll along the front with a rucksack of beers that I'd bribed the barman at the hotel to sell me (after he'd repeatedly told me that no alcohol was to be given to players, by order of the manager). Luckily for both of us, money talks in this part of the world; I slipped him the equivalent of about £2 and he happily set about filling my bag. I set off down the beach – which turned out to be a terrible idea. It was ridiculously hot and before long I retreated inland and hailed a cab.

"I'll take you somewhere nice," said the driver.

That was a worry. I was probably heading to a brothel, but in the absence of any other options or sun cream I jumped into the car and we zoomed off down a recently finished motorway. In the event he did take me somewhere nice – a marina with cafés, shops and a golf course about half an hour down the coast. It was stunning. I took a table outside a café and ordered a Coke. In the distance I could hear building work going on, and when I stood I realised that they were building out into the sea, similar to the Palm Islands in Dubai. All around me there were agents selling property for the area. As I was thinking about taking a look, a voice said, "I know you," and a hand shot out to be shaken.

"Jesus," I said. "What are you doing here?"

It was an estate agent from a property company that I've done a lot of business with over the years, and he was here selling apartments for the island that I could hear being built. After a couple of Cokes and his warm-up patter I agreed to take a car with him to see what they were doing. He explained that the newly added land was made up of four islands shaped like coral stretching far out to sea. There was nothing to see, of course, only small sand storms and giant boulders, but with a little imagination you could picture how beautiful it was going to be. Back in his pop-up shop he showed me models of the place and explained the tourism and business infrastructure that was coming to RAK. It sounded amazing, and I had already fallen for the place. He gave me the company bank details; I transferred £210,000 there and then and bought myself a two-bedroom penthouse overlooking the Arabian Sea. At least, I bought a picture of one.

Now, I appreciate that what I'm about to say may make me sound like a complete wanker, and I have no excuse. I'm merely telling you how it is. I completely forgot about that purchase until about a year ago, when out of the blue the agent phoned me and offered me £400,000 for the same apartment, even though it was still not finished (thanks mostly to the property crash).

Not bad, I thought, for something bought on a whim. Still, I fobbed him off, began to do some digging to work out what was going on – and made an amazing discovery. The island next to mine was now spoken for – by Real Madrid, who had announced that they were building a five-star hotel, apartments, villas, a training complex, a 10,000-seater stadium, a museum and a sporting academy. There were even rumours of a theme park. Why here, of all places? Well, the location is said to be equidistant from Europe and Madrid's enormous following in Asia.

Finally, after five years of swimming upstream through a torrent of shit, there was a bit of good news. Now I just have to decide whether to cash in or hold my nerve; whatever happens, I guarantee it'll have been the wrong choice. Anyway, it's a nice problem to have. I may not be able to do punditry there and I may not have a club to play for in this part of the world, but if everything goes completely tits-up, which it looks like it might, at least I'll still have a home of sorts.

I do have a few concerns about the area, though. When I got back to the hotel after my hard day's flat-buying I still had a rucksack of beers. So I got some ice from the bar, took a seat on the beach and called my room-mate, who came down in record time because it was almost impossible to get a beer out there thanks to our manager. We watched the sun go down and drank the beers until they had worked their magic and told us that we really ought to check out the local nightlife. There was one club nearby and it looked extremely "yocal", but when in Rome ...

On our way in the bouncer looked at us as if to say, "Really?" and gave me some abuse about my shoes, but for once I held my tongue. Inside we found that we were the only westerners in the place, but once the locals had had a good stare they began flashing us half-smiles that seemed to say, "Fair play for coming in. You're idiots but at least you've got balls."

Much later, two very attractive local ladies came and sat down on the same bench as us. This was great: clearly word had got out that we were footballers and the local females had bitten. We had a chat with them and made them laugh a bit but they wouldn't let us buy them any drinks. A little later we found out why, when two huge fellas arrived almost to a standing ovation and sat down next to these women. That was when I realised that people were laughing at us because we'd sat in the VIP section and clearly didn't belong there – at least not in this club. Just then the owner of the place came over and whispered to one of the men, who immediately turned to us and asked, "Who the fuck are you?"

It was time to go: the atmosphere had changed and people were leaving. We made a thousand apologies and tried to make tracks, but it was clear that we not going to be allowed to go quietly. The men stood up, and so did we; the women just sat there looking at us. I tried to apologise yet again, when one of the men pulled a knife and held it to my face. It must have been five or six inches long and had a wicked point. Nobody has ever pulled a knife on me before and, I'll be honest, I absolutely shat myself. I turned on my heel with my friend and bolted for the door with my hands in the air, which as you know is the universal sign for "I've fucked up and I'm sorry but we'll have no trouble here." Unfortunately they followed us and we had to run down the road. I had no idea where we were heading but I did hear the roar of engines starting outside the club, where moments before we'd darted past some very expensive Italian sports cars. There was only one thing to do, and that was hide. We jumped into an alley, where we found a bush protruding from the side of an old building. We were in that bush until 3am in the morning, being eaten alive by the nuclear mosquitoes that live out that way. Only then did we dare quickstep back to the hotel.

When I visit a new area I like to have a look around but it just goes to show that you don't have to go too far off the beaten track before you find trouble. By the sea I own a beautiful penthouse apartment with Real Madrid as my neighbours; down the road there are people who want to stab me. The whole thing sounds remarkably like the situation I left behind at the football club I was playing for at the time.

COULD I BE A COACH?

You know what puts me off coaching? Players like me – players who can't really be coached how to play, only what formation to play in and where to stand for set pieces. One of my former coaches made the fatal mistake of telling me that he didn't want to coach me because he loved the way I played and didn't want to change it. I took that as a huge compliment, whether it was meant that way or not, and began thinking that I was the finished article. The truth is, you never really stop learning; you only ever stop wanting to learn.

But that mindset hasn't stopped a couple of managers and owners asking me to come in and take up a coaching position. There is a bit of "jobs for the boys" about it, but that's how much of this game works, I'm afraid. And it never hurts to gain your coaching badges because opportunities don't stop presenting themselves and one day you might wake up a changed man and ready for the challenge. It's also very handy that the badges are heavily subsidised for footballers by the PFA. So I threw caution to the wind and took the plunge.

Choosing the place to do your Uefa coaching badges is really quite a free process. Anybody can take the course anywhere they like, providing they can put the hours in. The actual tuition takes place either at your club over the season or as a fast-track eight-day course, accompanied by a huge questionnaire asking you how you would set up your team in certain situations and what you would do to counter a team that was attacking you in a certain formation. Everybody I know copies the answers (even though there are no right or wrong responses) from the coach at the club who is trained to give the course. I have yet to meet a player who has done anything for himself from start to finish.

Years ago everybody wanted to take the badges in Ireland because it was an almighty piss-up, but as football has adopted a more serious approach that has changed. Now there are ex-players and players alike attending FA-led courses all over Britain, depending on where they're from or where they want to coach.

There are pros and cons to taking your badges in Wales or Scotland, just as there are for Northern Ireland and England, and because each nation's course is led by its FA, the way a person is coached varies according to the local football philosophy.

Most players I know choose to take the course in England because for some reason its FA is seen as more reputable, but there is a right place to take the course and a wrong place. One local supremo hates footballers, is bitter about having never been a footballer, and fails every footballer who takes it on the smallest of technicalities – basically if they don't agree with his approach. He would fail Mourinho given the chance, the idiot.

There are some other anomalies when it comes to coaching. A goalkeeper, for example, must have an outfield licence as well as a goalkeeper licence, even if he only coaches goalkeepers. You won't find a goalkeeper who is happy with that arrangement.

Anybody can apply to take the course, so that means that a man who coaches kids' football could find himself sharing a pitch with the great and good of the game, provided he can lay his hands on about £5,000 for the course. The mix of people that I saw included ex-players, current players, a guy who just wanted to coach his son's youth team, a guy who was coaching women goalkeepers, and plenty of people who were involved one way or another in the local community. But even if the amateurs' money is green, the treatment they receive from the tutors at the FA is markedly different. They will bend over backwards for the players and ex-players but they are certainly not as helpful with Joe Public.

On the pitch you have to wear a microphone so the tutors can hear you instructing the players, and you are filmed. The session itself breaks coaching down into three areas:

PHASE OF PLAY

Taking a session to emphasise phases of play might involve a three-quarter-length pitch that is full-width. In a session like this we might be trying to teach a specific midfielder to attack the opposition by running with the ball. We'd do this using a full-sized goal and playing 9 v 8. To start the session a player behind the goal might launch a ball to the halfway line to simulate a clearance. My chosen midfielder then controls it and starts his run. My defence would be pushing up to squeeze the space so the whole session becomes realistic.

On the B licence I would teach my midfielder to take the ball on his back foot and look around him to see where the space is, the opposition and his teammates. The idea is to help him choose the best place to take his first touch. Can he go forward? Does he go to the side? Does he need one or two touches? He needs to lift his head up and know where the space is immediately. Can he run into it? Should he play a one-two around an oncoming striker first?

It all depends what you are trying to achieve from the session and who you are trying to improve. In first-team situations, you might practise variations of this drill all week if you know that the opposition defence is slow at pushing out after an attack. As the coach, you decide how best to deal with a situation given to you by the tutor. Again, there are no wrong or right answers: if I feel that I have a talented midfielder who is very good at running with the ball at the opposition, then I can work on this. Somebody else may chose a different approach, but I pass or fail based on how I have set the session up, whether everybody understands, and whether or not I step in at the right moment to correct something that didn't work the first time round.

FUNCTIONS

This leads on to functions, which is the second aspect of coaching. This time we might only set up half a pitch with the aim of teaching our left-back how to stop crosses. Every coach and manager is different; for me, I'd like my left-back, where possible, to get to the ball as quickly as he can without "selling" himself, then show the winger away from the goal – down the line ideally – or better yet, get the winger to turn back so that my defence can squeeze up a few yards. Another coach might want his defender to show the winger on to his weak foot or encourage him to cross from deeper areas because he knows that he has two dominant centre-backs and a goalkeeper who will always come to catch the ball. It also depends on the left-back: is he quick, in which case he can get to the ball, or is he slow, in which case he has to try to stand the winger up and narrow the angle for the cross until he can get near enough to make a challenge or encourage him to pass back?

Depending on how a person wants to coach, the session might be set up in a variety of ways. You might choose for the opposition to start from a quick throw-in that the left-back has to get out to, or you might start from the left wing and shift the ball across the pitch to the right winger. Utimately the result is the same: the left-back has to stop the cross. You can expand on this by introducing an overlapping full-back to complicate things or a third man runner, a midfielder, who goes in behind the full-back as the ball is laid back.

In a first-team situation a coach or manager would work on this sort of thing during training just prior to a match against a big team. I can remember working on how to restrict the space in the full-back areas for a week before playing Arsenal at the Emirates. The answer is very simple: you don't come out of your shape. If everybody stays in their "hole", there is no space to run in behind. But there are so many little nuances to this. You'd have a striker on Arteta, for example, trying to pinch the ball from him and stop him from playing. You'd have your goalkeeper starting 10 yards off his line in case Cazorla slips a ball through that beats your back four. You'd have a deep-lying midfielder shielding every little two-yard movement that Giroud or Podolski makes so the ball cannot get through to them. And the biggest thing of all when playing against Arsenal is: never follow the ball, always follow the man. Much of Arsenal's success comes from one-twos around the box and balls slipped between the full-back and centre-half. Never ball-watch; always know where the man is. Sometimes it works: Wigan have had a fair amount of success, as have Swansea. How did we get on? They stuffed us. "C'est la vie," as they say in the Arsenal dressing room.

SMALL-SIDED GAMES

The small-sided games, traditionally seen as a bit of a jolly at the end of first-team training, are actually the most important aspect of taking your coaching badges because this is where everything that a coach has learned can be implemented in one session. It isn't just tactics – it's how you engage with the players and when you step in and correct something.

For the Uefa B licence the game will usually be 9 v 9. The tutor will give you a topic that he wants to see implemented in the small-sided game; nobody is supposed to know what that will be but most of us tend to find out a week or so in advance over a beer with the tutor. As I said, most tutors want to pass the players and ex-players who take the course, and offer them help above and beyond what is expected. For everyone else, they don't really care too much.

This is the main test of your coaching ability and the best thing to do is to go away and ask a couple of friends who are already in coaching for tips. Then you draw up a session plan: this needs to include the size of the pitch that you want to work on, how many players you need, what equipment you're going to use (ball, bibs, cones etc). And, of course, what session you plan to put on and what you are looking to achieve.

You'll also need to recognise the ability of the players who are available for the session. There is no point in writing a training plan that is beyond them. Most of the time you'll have a youth team to work with at the training ground; they will be fairly decent and well drilled, but if you are working with a very low-level, non-league club side, there is no point in saying that you are going to set up something that involves overlaps, third man runs and filling in because that won't be second nature to them. They may not even be fit enough to do it.

After determining how fit your team are and how quickly they are likely to get the hang of things, you set out a time frame. Twenty-five minutes is plenty for a small-sided game.

The first thing to do is to get all the players around you in a huddle on the pitch and outline your plan. Introduce yourself, name the teams and sort out your players. This has to be done really quickly because footballers soon lose interest. The amount of times I've been standing in these huddles and gone on to screensaver before hearing, "Right, everybody, take your places ..."

First you do two or three minutes' free play, then you go into the session and coach what you see – the directive from the English FA is to stop the session when you see something that needs addressing. Blow the whistle, step in and explain what the problem is before offering a demo and making sure that everybody understands. If somebody still doesn't understand, you replay the exact same thing again. If somebody gets it wrong again or still can't do what you're telling him, then get rid of him. That's my advice, by the way – not official FA protocol.

• • •

In these sessions you will be marked on the way you deliver your information; this is the part of coaching that a lot of footballers really don't appreciate. Whenever I talk to players who are about to take their badges, they always talk about having played for 15 or 20 years and knowing everything. In a way they do, but so many of them have no idea how to get what they know across to others – and that, after all, is coaching.

Broadly speaking, there are three styles of coaching: command; question-and answer; or both. Which you favour will depend on what sort of person you are and at what level you are coaching. When I coached our youth team during a Uefa B session I found that I was a combination of command and question-and-answer, but that was probably because you can be forceful with a youth team while encouraging them to participate in the answers.

Let's go back to the left-back trying to stop crosses: if you're a person who coaches command-style, then you might talk to your full-back like this: "Look, if the wide man is running down the wing I want you to show him down the line. Don't let him inside; get your body shape right like this and watch the ball. That's what I want. OK, play." If the winger does happen to get the cross in, you would stop the session and say something like, "Right, when the wide man gets into a position to cross, I want you to get tighter to him and stop that ball. Don't stand off him – stop the cross and force him back. That's what I want. OK, play."

If you go for the question-and-answer approach, however, you'd talk to your left-back like this: "How close do you want to get to him? Do you think that your body shape is right here? Why do you want to show him inside? Could you be closer there? Why not?"

A combination of these approaches seems to work best, especially at first-team level. You don't want to boss seasoned professionals around, or to talk to them as if they're idiots. After all, they see what you're trying to tell them up close on the pitch every week.

And at first-team level you also need to start dealing with egos. I have seen some of the most enthusiastic coaches in the game come into a club fresh from the FA's coaching course with all the enthusiasm and ideas that you'd expect, only for the team to feel as if they are being treated like youth team players. One of two things happen: the players don't respond and the coach leaves; or, far more common, the coach stops being so busy and fits in with the approach that already exists at the club. Remember, we're talking about coaches. It's different when a new manager comes in – everybody is on their best behaviour and generally does what is asked of them.

The Uefa A licence is more about 11 v 11, and here it can make a difference where you take the course. As a friend told me, "Some of the other nations are said to be easier: they want you to pass the course so there's more help available. But in the English version the FA are right up their own arse and they absolutely will not bend. It's more like a declaration, 'We're the FA and this is how we do things.'"

At this level the scenarios given to a coach are very specific and on a full-size scale. So your tutor might give you a topic such as team pressing and sitting back, and then he'll give you a specific scenario. So for the above topic he might say, "Right, you need to get the ball back but you're 1-0 down with five minutes to play – go!" Then you need to coach the players for that scenario, so obviously you're going to press the life out the opposition to win the ball back. You might even sacrifice a man at the back and go to a three to help the midfield and forwards press.

The FA are very big on zones, such as where the ball is delivered from and where it is cleared to. They seem to place quite a lot of faith in these statistics, and I've heard that they do a lot of statistical research themselves. Most of the research that goes in to the A licence comes from games at the World Cup, the Champions League and the Premier League. This means that the whole licence is based on the elite in the game, which is fine, but what about the guy who goes back to Rochdale in League One where every other goal has come from a set piece that hasn't been covered? That's why the A licence really isn't essential. I believe the B licence is the right way to go because it gives you a good grounding while allowing you to put your own unique approach and ideas over the framework. Otherwise you might as well be a robot.

Last year I took a walk over to the youth team pitches to talk to the manager. He's a good guy who really cares about the way the kids learn their trade and he was very helpful when I asked him about the path I could follow in coaching. I've told him that I'm not overly keen but he has been very persuasive in encouraging me to get involved, and in fairness I have always preached that there is a lot of knowledge wasted in this game when players simply retire. I remember talking to him about it during one of his youth team training sessions.

He turned to me and said, "Look, it isn't rocket science. They're kids. You have to teach them the basics and then keep improving them as quickly as you can so that they're ready for the first team, while accepting that only a couple will make it. The most important part of coaching these kids is how you deal with them, how you treat them and how you get your point across. What do you think is the worst thing you could say to one of these kids during a session?"

I thought for a minute. I thought about what I wouldn't want to hear from a coach whose playing career was of next to no interest to me. Then it came to me. I had no idea if it was the answer he was looking for. After all, you could tell one of them that their mum has just died, couldn't you? That would be a bit of a morale-crusher.

"'In my day we did it like this,'" I said.

"Fuck me, lad," he said. "We might just make a coach of you yet."

COULD I BE A DIRECTOR
OF FOOTBALL?

Of all the jobs in the game that a footballer can do when he finishes his playing career, director of football is one that I have always fancied – and I think I'd be good at it. As with many jobs, you need to serve an apprenticeship, which is another way of saying that the money you earn will be crap while you prove yourself. In the summer I was offered the chance to come into a good-sized club and train under the existing director of football – something that I mulled over for a very long time.

As a player you can tell a good director of football by how happy everyone is with your contract terms. If you sign your contract, then in principle you are happy, but it isn't quite as simple as that and a good director of football will have secured you for not a penny more than he had to, so that – in theory at least – the chairman and the fans are happy too.

It suits me because I'm a pretty good negotiator and I know the market rate of most players. But there is far more to it than that: it is a job that requires you to be at the beck and call of just about everybody linked with the club, from board level through to players and their agents and the scouting system. That last one is particularly important, because yours is perhaps the only job in the game that is completely dictated by budgets, and balancing transfer and wage budgets can be tricky when people around you are trying to convince you to sign the next best thing. You need to be principled and have a lot of faith in yourself.

And there is another string to the bow, too. You are involved in a lot of the hiring and firing that goes on at the club and, as you know, the turnover of staff within a football club is both considerable and frequent. And that is the part that appeals to me: of all the jobs in this game, a director of football has a chance to build something from the ground up. Providing he can sell it to his owner, he has a chance to go into a club and lay out a blueprint for the future. That involves picking a manager who will play the new style of football, on the budget that you have determined, with players you have chosen to sign, on the recommendation of scouts that you employed. You cannot overstate the importance of a good director of football, and mark my words, behind every half-decent manager there is a talented chief executive or director of football subtly pulling the strings. I don't care what level of the game it's at or who the manager is – it's a fact of football.

And I think I'd be good at that. I think I'd be very good at getting rid of the dead wood and starting again, and I love the idea of building a football club up from an also-ran into a force that is recognised around the world. I have the same naivety and blind faith in myself for this job as I did when I became a player. Why not become a manager? Because I don't want to deal with the players, I don't want to deal with tactics. Those are not my strengths.

So I made a few calls, all of which produced the same initial response, namely that I was too young to be a director of football. It made all the times that I've heard those same people say "If you're good enough, you're old enough" appear a little hollow, to say the least. But it's true that I have never hired or fired a manager. I've tried my best to get rid of one or two, of course, but I never officially had the power to make it happen.

Fortunately, when my peers were turning left to talk to celebrities, I was turning right to talk to the people in suits. The result is that I know an awful lot of people who have important jobs and who like mixing with the common folk from time to time. Some of these guys own football clubs and are more than happy to share their wisdom with me.

The first person I met up with was the director of football of a big club. He'd previously been *my* director of football. He was really supportive even when I told him that his job would be perfect for me.

"When we signed you, what did I tell you over the phone?" he said.

"You said how much you wanted me to sign and that the manager was going to build a team around me," I said.

"So there you are," he said. "It's the little things that are important. You're like the UN. You meet people, negotiate, try to make sure everybody is happy, while always remembering what numbers you have to play with. Never, ever, forget about budget, no matter how badly you want to sign a player. I can tell you why you'd make a good director of football. Can you remember what you said to me on the phone when I offered you the first deal?"

I laughed. I certainly could. "I told you it was a piss-take and that I wouldn't sign for less than double that."

"Exactly, and you were how old, 20-something? You're the only player who has ever negotiated with me. It's natural for you and you ended up with more. So there you go. You can do this job – you'd be good at it."

"Yeah, I remember all that now," I said. "Either I'm good or you're lucky to be in the job."

"Well, there is that," he said. "You were a fantastic player and exactly what we wanted. I'd probably have gone to an extra £5,000 a week, actually."

"Yes, well, you would say that now, wouldn't you? I'll tell you what I do remember," I said. "Negotiating the player bonuses with you."

He turned, stony-faced, "Yes, you nearly cost me my job over that. The chairman was furious."

Years ago, as I mentioned briefly in I Am The Secret Footballer, I led a player revolt over a paltry player bonus sheet that the club offered us based on Premier League survival. It was late in pre-season and the team photograph was our last bargaining tool. I was determined to make it count. I'm not sure why the club's hierarchy were so worried about a team photograph, but they were. It must have been because all the sponsors were there waiting for their snap with the team. On team photo days, you don't just have one shot and go home – you're there all afternoon having individual snapshots, head shots and personal shots, signing things, giving interviews and so on, and every affiliate of the club sends a delegation to the stadium to have their own shot with the squad. So if you're sponsored by Samsung or DHL, those companies will send a delegation of half a dozen people to mingle and have their own individual squad photo. And so it goes on: kit manufacturers, training ground sponsors, match day catering delegations, stand sponsors, stadium sponsors, "friends of the club" ...

They were all there, and now that I think about it, our actions would probably have painted the club in an awful light if the standoff had continued much longer.

As we sat in the club reception area I told the players that if we all stuck together we'd be fine. Our captain did his usual trick and left us to it but I stood firm, much to the annoyance of our director of football, who was in quite a panic at this point. First he threatened to fine all of us but we refused to budge. I sent all the young players and first-year pros out on to the pitch where the photos were being taken, so that their reputations would remain intact. You should never involve the young lads in these sorts of negotiations – it isn't fair on them, and in any case it is the job of the older pros to watch

139

out for them. With the bulk of the first-team squad standing firm, the director of football returned with an offer.

"OK," he said, "here's your deal. Sign it, and if you're not out on the pitch in the next five minutes I'm sacking all of you." Now, that would have been a good story, but in the interests of harmony I made everyone sign the agreement; the outcome was that at the end of the season we were all at least £50,000 better off and some players who had played in all the games doubled that. I didn't get any thanks for negotiating that deal but I did get a cheque, and that was always the name of the game.

Dinner was winding down and I paid the bill with my usual dry humour. "No, please," I said. "After I make a club hundreds of millions of pounds I like to buy them dinner too."

"You're still a bloody idiot," said the director of football. "Can you remember what you said to me when we were negotiating that bonus deal?"

"Not really," I said,

"You said to me, 'We're not gonna bend over and take it up the arse any more.' I had to look serious but when I left the room I absolutely pissed myself. If you do take up the role, I'm looking forward to dealing with you."

"As if I'd want any of your players," I said.

"Stay in touch, mate," he said. "And good luck with it."

As I've said before, if you're going to do something you really need to immerse yourself in it. That approach stems from the most successful period of my playing career, in which I really did sacrifice everything to become a winner.

So as I was thinking about this latest offer I called a good friend of mine who sits on the board of a huge club and is in charge of appointing managers. I know a lot about football, but this is a process whose finer points are still a mystery to me. It was a bit of a coup to get him to talk, because there are very few people who will tell you how they hire and fire managers.

We met at a restaurant in Manchester; a place that he told me had been very popular with the last manager. He'd bought an impressive amount of literature with him and presented it to me at the table after looking around to make sure there was nobody looking over at us. "Before we start," he said, "my name is nowhere near this, OK? Seriously, if one person finds out, that's it for us." Some people have no faith.

He'd been working on bringing in the right manager for some time and the whole thing had become a bit of a saga as far as the media were concerned.

"At this level there is a huge amount of negotiation that you need to account for," he told me. "Negotiation with the club, the manager, the agent, your board, the media. Sometimes I think all I do is negotiate. What irritates me is that we all know what the outcome is going to be – we're going to get the man we want because of who we are – but we always have to go through this mating dance first. When I first took the job I didn't want to upset anybody, so I was perhaps too nice and I'd let the situation play out. But now that I'm more experienced, or possibly just because of who we are and the fact that I'm old and grumpy, I am a lot more comfortable in saying, 'Right, this is your last chance – you either want the job or you don't.' And the great by-product of that approach is that the manager begins to panic and starts lobbying his existing club to let him go and waiving all sorts of bonuses and monies that he's owed as a result. He thinks he's helping you out but you've really worked him from behind. It's all about knowing when to play your best cards.

"It's much easier now: the pool of people that we would interview is much smaller than it used to be because the remit is very simple – success. But things haven't always been as easy and colleagues of mine at League One and Two clubs are really struggling in the same job. The financial fair play rules are affecting their choices every day, including which manager they bring in."

He took out a binder with "Job Description" written on the front, apparently borrowed from a friend at another club. "This is what a club would typically send to any manager who applied for the job. They might not even get the courtesy of an interview but they would still get a copy of this." The job description set out what was required of any new manager, and it wasn't simply a case of listing the basics, such as, "in charge of first-team affairs and arrives for work in a punctual fashion" (although that was on there, believe it or not). According to this document, the manager was expected to attend all technical board meetings, manage the team budget (far more common the lower down you go), and to have Uefa A, B and Pro licences and a proven and profitable track record in player trading.

Then he showed me a five-year business plan that he'd borrowed from the same colleague. "This is what I mean regarding the financial fair play rules," he said. "Let me take you through this. This business plan is designed to get their club into the top half of the Premier League from where they are now within five years, while having to adhere to the fair play rules. This document is shown to prospective managers at the interview stage and presented by the director of football or chief executive. Clubs at that level really have to marry their ambitions to those of any new manager, especially now; they have to share the ideal more than at our level. At our level we supply the manager with everything he needs; at that level the manager is much more hands on and needs to be fully acquainted with budgets, for example."

The start of the business plan lists various facets of the club – football, business, community etc – then talks about each one. The first is obviously football: they want to get to the Premier League in five years and the way they have decided to do it is dictated by budget. The board have decided that the most effective way to achieve their goal is to introduce a "club culture" that boils down to exploiting the products of their youth team by playing them in the first team for one year and then selling them and putting the money back into the academy. Because of the financial fair play model, they see this as their best chance.

Further into the booklet – which is pretty hefty, I have to say – they talk about creating an environment to succeed. Unusually, the chain of command has the manager and the director of football together at the top, with the technical board below them (head of sports science, academy manager etc), and then the club board below them. There are two plans for success based on promotions and financial gains; if the first fails, plan B kicks in immediately. These plans are accompanied by details of how the transition of the squad fits in, and provide for slashing budgets should the team fail to win promotion. They also allow for more money to be made available if they do go up. Wherever money is tight, the youth team have a much larger slice of the pie. The budget for the squad is split between starters, cover players and youth team players and the idea is to have a mixture of all three in the starting 11 positions on the pitch.

Next to each of those positions is the budget. The starting players are expected to earn between £1,500 and £2,500 a week, with the cover players earning £1,000 to £1,499 and the youth team players between £100 and £250. A chart shows how their value to the club diminishes and when the club should look to cash in on any given player based on age and standing. This model goes on right up to the Premier League.

Halfway through the presentation is a very simple five-point plan explaining that players who come into the club need to be identified, scouted and analysed, targeted and then purchased before being integrated with the first team and their new surroundings. Believe me, although that sounds simple, I have played for big clubs where foreign players with no English have been bought in and then left to fend for themselves on day one.

Then it moves on to the make-up of the squad, and unfortunately this part of the plan has a very clear message for players like me. At the top of the page under the heading "Young Players", it simply says three things: "young, hungry, talented". At the bottom of the page it says: "Do not sign or retain cover players over the age of 26." The importance of the academy players is emphasised everywhere: in League Two they expect at least 20 per cent of the first team to be made up of youth team graduates; in League One the figure falls to 15 per cent; in the Championship the figure is 10 per cent; and in the Premier League it falls to 3 per cent. This may sound like a huge tail-off but there are market forces at work here. The academy isn't just a way of supplementing the first team; it is a way of supplementing the business model up to the Premier League, but in the top division the income is so vast that the model changes. A Premier League club can sell its youth team players to a huge amount of clubs even if they are not good enough for their own first team because it has probably canvassed them from around the world. In the lower leagues the youth team players are likely to be local players, with perhaps only one or two capable of playing professionally.

"Now take a look at some of the CVs they received," my friend said. "The manager that my friend's club really wanted was already working elsewhere, which wasn't really a problem because the possibility of an acquisition was in the budget. They asked him to send a CV through as a matter of course, and this is what turned up." With that he brought out a single sheet of A4 paper that appeared to have been faxed and that stated only the more memorable achievements of the man's playing career. "Now compare that CV to this guy's" – and he pulled out what looked like a very comprehensive holiday brochure. "This is 50 pages long," said my friend, "and the detail is ridiculous. He talks about his approach to strength and conditioning, the medical side, tactics, pre-season, nutrition, psychology, motivation, even the welfare of the players' families. Jesus Christ, it's no wonder he didn't get an interview. Who has the time to read all that when you have 200 CVs to get through?

"At my friend's club – and this is happening more and more – the interview was split into two parts: a football side that focused on tactics and a financial side that dealt with the budget. The tactical side was incredibly simple, and although each manager had the chance to put across his philosophy, it really boiled down to one question that was posed to everyone: 'How important are set pieces?' Now, that sounds really amateur but it is in fact incredibly clever. When Albert Roux interviews graduate chefs, he doesn't ask for a three-Michelin-starred dinner – he asks them to cook him an egg. If they think it's beneath them they don't get past the interview, but if they treat it with respect they get the job. Genius.

"The answers that came back could tell you everything about a manager. One of them said, 'Yes, they are important. I would send my centre-halves up for corners and I would bring a striker back to defend them.' The guy who got the job said something like, 'Incredibly important – over half the goals in Leagues One and Two came from set pieces last year but you scored only 23 per cent of your goals from set pieces, which puts you 14th in the league. You need to be at least sixth for automatic promotion, and this is how I am going to change those stats. You also conceded 35 per cent of your goals from corners and crosses that had been cleared. Twenty-five per cent of those crosses landed between your right-back and your right-sided centre-half, and these are the players that I have identified to replace them, plus a left-back who is not stopping crosses well enough. If we can reduce this figure to 10 per cent, that puts us fifth in that particular table of statistics, which is where we need to be to guarantee automatic promotion.'

"Now, that's a proper answer. In one question he had demonstrated that he knew the league and that he knew the players that he could get for the budget that he was going to be given. He had also targeted promotion from day one.

"Incidentally," he said, "most managers are becoming incredibly big on recovery the lower down you go, in a bid to improve professionalism. They are giving players fewer days off because a lot of them sit on the sofa in a bad position and drink fizzy drinks and eat shit. At least if they are in on Sundays then they can recover for a few hours.

"Anyway, the financial interview was much more detailed: it had to be because finances in the lower leagues are becoming so much more important. He asked them about social media, such as Twitter and Facebook; given recent experiences, he wanted to know how they'd deal with disciplining a player who abused that privilege. Most of the managers said they would have no hesitation in fining or even sacking a player, and that is what my friend wanted to hear.

"I've met the guy that my friend appointed and he seems to be on the level – young, ambitious and very knowledgeable. We sat around over dinner and there seemed to be a good natural fit between his approach and the club."

"So what about you guys?" I said. "How did you go about identifying the right manager?"

"Well we're different. We can pretty much have our pick, so the pool is reduced to perhaps five or six names. At the level that you'll start from you'd be much better off thinking about the situation that your club is in. It really depends where the club finds itself. I have been in situations where the club has been third bottom of the Premier League and we needed somebody who could come in and manage for 10 games in two or three weeks. That is completely different – that is what happened at Sunderland. They paid him a fortune to keep them up and guaranteed him all three years' money if they sacked him thereafter. People said it was reckless but those people don't understand football as a business – it was £5m against £100m. They chose Di Canio because they needed maximum uplift at the club for the last few games. There was no point in bringing in a manager with a five-year plan: they needed a short-term solution.

"At the end of the season you've got two months and you can assess the club's situation because you know what league you're in. Our biggest regret was keeping the manager that we got promoted with, because we should have replaced him and restructured the whole squad. We should have lost some of the senior players who got us promoted – remember, you don't owe them anything – and bought in talented and hungry players. When you get promoted through the leagues, unless you have a young, forward-thinking, intellectual manager, you pretty much need to transition the squad as you go, particularly from the Championship to the Premier League.

"And don't be afraid to change manager. Changing manager is not a big deal any more because winning something is not the name of the game for many clubs now. Winning is staying in the Premier League and trying not to lose too much money.

"Balancing the books is still important, especially when the financial fair play model comes into full force in the Premier League. The problem with the cavalier approach is that you can get caught with two or three players whom you don't want and who are earning big money. Astute management can get those players out – it's simply a combination of the chief executive and chief of recruitment working with the manager. We've got one player earning a fortune at the moment that we don't want and who still has one year left on his deal. The manager needs to speak to him properly in order to get the most out of him and make sure that he doesn't become a troublemaker, but always with the end game in mind that we need to get him out. Where you're starting from, it will be easier if you get promoted, because players are so much easier to move on with 'promoted' on their CVs, especially strikers. You'll always find a manager at another club who thinks he can get more out of the player than you can. Managers need to be more ruthless when they are promoted to the Premier League – the cull needs to be much bigger than it currently is.

"The reason we were hammered by the media in the summer was simply that we were going to be the biggest off-field story in the press and the press wanted the story as soon as possible because they had nothing to write about. They began to make things up about managers rejecting us and fall-outs within the club – that's what they do. In the summer when a club is looking for a manager you've got more time to consider what you need, but the media play on the fans' anxiousness. The truth is that people only see what happens on the field, but off the field there is a huge amount of activity that goes on. The commercial activity of marketing and selling season tickets, for example – that is an opportunity to ensure your income for the whole year. As soon as the transfer window opens the fans want to see player trading, so we prepare for that.

"On the subject of season tickets, let me give you a friendly piece of advice. Never, ever factor in your season ticket money. My old club once did it in the summer before they got relegated and it was a huge mistake. We needed instant cash for the manager to buy the players that he needed in January because we waited so long before appointing a manager and missed most of the summer window. All of that could have been avoided by appointing a manager in a timely fashion."

The evening was winding down and I was very grateful to my friend and indeed *his* friend for allowing me to see exactly how things are done. But I couldn't help thinking that he still hadn't told me much about how his own club were getting on with replacing their manager. So I made a last appeal.

"Look," he said. "The reason I'm not telling you anything about our own situation is that it's completely different from where you'll be starting from. At this level our biggest problem is media intrusion. It's very aggressive and could scupper my ability to get the right guy. If too much is said in the media before we make the appointment, then any manager could be put off by that. Loose lips sink ships.

"I knew maybe 18 months ago that we were going to change manager this summer and I have been preparing for it ever since by culling the squad, refusing transfer targets, restricting budgets and all the time putting out feelers to the right people to gauge initial interest. We have to be careful from an ownership point of view, too: we don't want to upset anybody who has a lot of money at risk with the club. At this level it is all about negotiating: every decision I make affects every other facet of the club in a way that is almost too much to comprehend at times. If I cut the budget, the manager immediately knows something is up. He loses motivation, the players lose motivation, the team begins to underperform and the fans lose heart, and all the time you just want to scream, 'This is what's happening, there is a reason,' but you can't. Do yourself a favour, mate – keep playing for as long as you can."

"OK," I said. "Last thing: did you get any applications for the job from the Championship manager brigade?'

"We had a few and we always send a nice letter politely declining their services but pointing out that their achievements are not to be sniffed at."

So there you have it.

COULD I BE A MANAGER?

As I've said before, I'm really not sure that management is for me. I'm intrigued by it and I like to think that I know what I'm doing, but I don't think I want to be the visible face of a football club any more. I can't be doing with having to answer to people who know less than me, like the media or the idiots who shout things out. My tolerance for all that died many years ago. I'd love to be involved in a club – the bigger the better – but my preference is to help pull the strings far away from the public gaze.

I remember parading a trophy around the pitch once when my manager walked up behind me and said, "Enjoy it – all these people will be calling for our heads next year." He was laughing and so was I because I was too caught up in the moment to take anything that anybody said seriously, but I've never forgotten it and I now know exactly what he meant. Management isn't about what you did for a club last season, or even last month – it's about what you're doing today. I'm not sure I have the stomach for that. I've been looking forward to enjoying my life for many years and even if I do end up having to hand it back for a while, I'm certainly not going to hand it over quite so easily this time.

But it isn't just that: as a player you can go home at a reasonable hour, while a manager should be first in and last out. He ought to set the example for how the players conduct themselves. The good ones do but some of them don't, whether it's the manager who doesn't turn up until Friday or the manager who is simply out of his depth.

I once played under a man who harboured so much jealousy about his players' financial success that he used it as the basis for almost every argument or dressing-down that he had with them, or even as the start of a conversation. He had never earned big money like we had, and clearly it irritated him. When everything was going well, he'd try to be everyone's best friend, to the point that he was cracking jokes in the tunnel with us before the game; but when we came back in at half time a goal down he'd bollock us, even though it was clear to any sane person that he'd played a part in taking our minds off the game. And he bollocked us in the worst way possible, by turning to his favourite subject. He'd claim that with the amount we earned in wages we ought to be winning every game. Football doesn't work like that, as I'm sure you know, but it does offer conclusive proof that you too can be a manager, even if you know nothing. I can even remember one team talk that started with, "Look, we've all got a bit of money, haven't we?" Nobody said a word. "Well, let's not kid ourselves," he laboured. "We have, haven't we?" Trust me, people who are obsessed with talking about money often have far less than they'd have you believe.

One season we went to Spain on an ill-thought-out trip that seemed to have no other justification than using up the budget. We didn't train, we barely exercised – we had a jog one morning – and it was basically a stag party. Upon arriving at the hotel, the manager gave a speech in which he said, "It's late, you've been on a plane, you need your rest and you'll get a night out later in the week." An hour later we were climbing over the spiked fence that surrounded the hotel. We hopped over one at a time until I realised that the key cards to our rooms also worked in the gate at the end of the path. As a side note, don't slam the gate when your team-mate has his testicles two inches above a spike – it's very painful.

Anyway, we went out and I have to say it was a really funny night that did wonders for team morale. Unfortunately the next night when we all went out together, the manager included, we inexcusably wandered past the previous night's bar. A rep came running out, shouting, "It's the guys from last night!" We went into the bar but the manager sat at the back and didn't say a word. He was absolutely gutted because he thought we were all his mates and wouldn't do that to him. He sat there without saying a word and I actually thought he was going to cry.

Eventually, our captain went to him and apologised, and later we all said sorry. I don't condone going out and disobeying the manager's orders. It isn't the right thing to do. In fairness, the young lads who tried to tag along with us were sent back with their tails between their legs for their own good, and it is also worth pointing out that a manager who commands respect would never be on the receiving end of behaviour like that. Still, I have no defence really; it wasn't professional, even if it was a great night.

On a personal level, the two of us really had our battles. We locked horns on numerous occasions – before matches, at half time, post-match and on the training ground – mainly because I was too clever for my own good and he was so rubbish at his job. One incident, however, really stands out. My little boy had been unwell for a few weeks. Nobody really knew what was wrong with him, but he was off his food, had become very quiet and withdrawn and didn't speak. He was constantly tired and lethargic. I took him to the doctor once and the hospital around the corner twice within a 10-day period and was told each time that nothing was wrong and that a scan or x-ray was a waste of time. We never made it past the on-duty doctor. Then one Friday evening while I was with the team for an away match, my wife rang from A&E and told me that a couple of hours earlier our son had collapsed at home and had been rushed into hospital, struggling to breathe.

There was an agonising wait. We were playing at the other end of the country and it was late at night. I was stuck far away from home and my head was all over the place. The manager was great. He said I was free to do whatever I wanted – nobody would think any less of me if I wanted to give the game a miss and go home to be with my son. I waited for the next call from my wife, and later that night she told me that he had been diagnosed with pneumonia and was now on a drip and responding well. They were keeping him in for three days until he was strong enough to go home, and after that he'd have to come back every week for eight weeks.

She sent me a picture of him laid out in a hospital bed on a drip, and I fell apart. He was so little and looked like he'd been knocked sideways. But he's a real fighter. When he was born he wasn't breathing and the medical staff had saved his life right in front of us, in the longest five minutes of my life. He's our little miracle man. Still, he could do without getting poorly all the time, the bloody idiot.

It seemed as if he was going to be OK, so I played the game and we actually won. I played pretty well considering everything that had happened, but by the end of the match I was starting to feel a bit emotional. After the game I checked my phone and my wife had sent me a few more pictures. I found a quiet corner of the changing room where the showers were, just out of sight of the manager giving his post-match speech, and that is where I bowed my head and discreetly shed a few tears.

The trouble came a few weeks later. The manager had been first class when my son fell ill and had offered me all the help in the world – something that I am grateful for – but he threw it all in my face during a half-time team talk in a match where we were being completely outplayed. He went around each player and lambasted each of us for our lack of effort. It was totally deserved because we had been shocking in that first half. When he got to me he let me have it with both barrels. That was fine because I had no excuse but he finished by saying, "Are you gonna fucking fight? Your little boy fought harder than you in the hospital."

The emotions from that episode were still very raw and I completely lost the plot. The entire changing room became involved in a battle to break the two of us apart. In the second half we went out and played better but the game had already been lost. The manager gave a big speech about how we had "tossed the game off" just to spite him, which was bollocks, but his standing at the club had crashed the moment that the words about my son left his lips. Many of the players with families, especially the foreign players for some reason, had found his words offensive and told me so on the journey home. The writing was on the wall for him.

The next season the club took a turn for the worse. The word was that the manager was two games away from the sack. I don't think the players had any intention of winning those two games on his behalf. But the footballing gods work in mysterious ways and before he could get the chop another club came in and not only poached him – something that ended badly – but paid hundreds of thousands of pounds in compensation, although a quick call to any one of our players would have told them that everyone would be glad to see the back of him. Football is a crazy business. There are too many people in positions of power who don't understand business. Some of them don't even understand football.

With the club in meltdown, our manager called a team meeting early one morning. The changing rooms at the training ground were in the usual horseshoe shape, facing some cupboards along the back wall where the kit man kept the towels. I was one of the last to file in that morning and I walked into a crowded changing room, staff included, with the manager sitting atop the towel cupboards swinging his feet with his head bowed. The last stragglers joined us, one of the coaches shut the door and the manager lifted his head. He was crying and looked as if he had been doing so all morning. He drew a couple of very deep breaths and rallied himself for his big moment. "Come on, ya cunt," he said under his breath, before rambling on about what a loyal man he was and how he had never jumped ship before but on this occasion he "had to look after himself".

It was nauseating. I don't have a lot of time for that sort of thing: if you're going, just go. Don't sit there with crocodile tears telling us how sorry you are when your players are facing a fucking shit storm. I hated the whole experience. Then he jumped down and walked around all the players, shook our hands and gave each of us an embarrassing little pep talk. I don't even remember what he said to me but I do remember thinking it was pretty rich to hand out so much advice just before leaving the recipients in the shit.

Later in the season that manager brought his new team back to play us in a league match and endured one of those days that everybody in football dreads. He was jeered and harassed all night and his team got "pumped", as we say in the trade. I shook hands with the opposition players and went to walk down the tunnel but our kit man grabbed me. "He's waiting for you in there," he said. "Stay with me when we go in." So I did, and sure enough there he was, waiting in the tunnel. He just stared at me and I at him, then he said, "Got your mates with you, have ya?" to which I replied, "No mates in football, gaffer. You should know that." It was true, but it did nothing to ease the tension.

After we'd got changed and left the stadium I took a call from our right-back.

"Mate, did you speak to the old gaffer?" he said.

"Only when I came off the pitch," I replied. "Why?"

"He's after you, pal. I just thought you should know that as I was in the car park leaving the stadium, he came running up and shouted, 'Where is that cunt?' I told him that you'd gone home and he said, 'Tell him from me that if I ever see him out I'll fucking stab him.'"

I immediately asked if my team-mate would be prepared to tell that tale to a journalist I knew. He wasn't, and I couldn't blame him, but it was worth a try.

He was a very insecure man and an extreme example of a flawed manager, but the truth is he wasn't helped by any of us. For example, I remember one occasion when the players had finished training and were having some banter on BB Messenger. The conversation became quite heated between a player who was on loan with us and another first-team player. It finally combusted when the loan player taunted the other man about his wife getting it "up the arse" from another player.

That comment lead to an almighty change in the atmosphere around the club. The manager had to put the two on the same five-a-side team in training even though they wouldn't pass to each other, because the alternative was that they went on opposite teams and tried to break each other's legs.

That's the sort of rubbish that you have to deal with as a manager, and at the worst clubs there are five or six examples of disharmony at any one time, with the potential for more. I'm not sure that I'd have time for that sort of thing as a manager. If it were all about playing football, then I might be interested, but dealing with the media, the owners, the fans and, above all, the players is not something that I could tolerate for any great length of time. But, more than any of that, I would hate to have a player like me in my squad because the time and effort that managers have had to put into me is not something that I could supply.

• • •

There are managers who don't help themselves, of course, and you never really know how you will turn out until you step into the big seat. That is another concern of mine, because I don't want to end up hating myself. What if I ended up like the manager at another club, who never seems to get tired of trumping his last crazy moment? A friend has told me many, many stories about him over the years.

One morning, apparently, as the squad was having breakfast in the canteen the manager called an impromptu set-piece session in front of the whiteboard along one side of the room.

He draws a large goal and says, "Right, where's my corner taker?" A lonely figure at the back eating toast puts his hand in the air. "Well, fuck off into the corner, then," says his manager. The lad gets up and wanders over to the corner of the room. "Hold on," says the manager. Take your ball with you – use the toast." Everyone in the canteen looks puzzled but sure enough the lad picks up his toast and takes it to the corner of the room. "Right," says the manager again. "Where's my one, two and three?" These are the players who make their runs across the near post, the middle and the far post as the ball is delivered. Three more arms nervously stretch toward the ceiling. "Come on, then," says the manager. "We haven't got all day. Move the tables out of the way ... Right, there's the penalty spot where you start from. OK, take the corner, then," he shouts to the lad holding the plate of toast. Nothing happens.

"Take the fucking corner! What are you, a fucking spastic? Frisbee the fucking toast! You're aiming for me." And he sticks his arms up in the air. The lad half-heartedly throws a piece of toast underarm towards his manager.

"Right, fuck off. Go and sit down. Give me the toast," says the manager. "Here's how to take a fucking corner. Ready ... HEAD IT!" and he frisbees a piece of toast from the corner of the room towards the three lads running towards the white-board. Amazingly, one of them glances it.

"TIMINGS!" shouts the manager. "Let's get our timings right!" He frisbees another piece; this time his centre-half connects with it and it hits the whiteboard. "PERFECT!" he shouts. "OK, no more of those. Right, where's my corner taker? You can watch from the stand this Saturday and you'll be practising corners all week with me."

Yes, he actually dropped one of his players for not frisbeeing a slice of toast across a canteen so that three lads could head it against a whiteboard. If nothing else, it's a first, and possibly a last. Scarily, that manager is still out there – and doing pretty well, as it happens.

And he isn't alone. There's another manager that I know of who, while not typically eccentric, is nonetheless somebody I wouldn't want to play for. I first heard of him a couple of years ago when somebody told me that his players were training from 9am to 5pm, which is unheard of. You may have a foreign manager who likes to do an afternoon session every now and again, and you can see how well that went down at Manchester City when Mancini tried to do it, but training typically starts at 10.30am and finishes around 12.30pm. Now, that may not sound like a long time, but working flat out for two hours takes it out of you and you need each afternoon to recover. And since the object of training is to win a football match at the end of the week, you need to leave enough in the tank to make sure the team performs at its highest level.

So starting at 9am and finishing at 5pm is rare for a reason – it's bloody ridiculous. I was also told that he sends text messages to his players to tell them whether or not they're playing; it's just unbelievable. One of the worst stories I've heard about this man is that when my friend went to meet him to discuss the possibility of signing for the club, he was kept waiting for two hours. When the manager came upstairs, it turned out that he'd been in the building the whole time. "Good, you're still here," he said. "That shows me that you want to play for this football club." What a cock – the fact that my friend had turned up to the meeting was a good indication too, I would have thought. When he phoned me later, I couldn't believe what I was hearing. "You're not signing for him, are you?" I asked. "No chance," said my friend. "He's off his head. Nine to five – what the fuck is that about?"

One of my old clubs experienced a meteoric rise from no-hopers to FA Cup winners, and there were still a few lads there who had been with them through thick and thin. It was always nice to listen to their stories because until you rock up at a club, much of what you know about it is only rumour and Chinese whispers. They told me that during one training session one of their ex-managers lost his rag with a centre-half because the striker on the other team kept winning headers in front of him from goal kicks. "Right," said the manager. "Clearly, you can't head the fucking ball, so head the back of his head."

This is a well-known piece of gamesmanship: if you can't head the ball but know that if your opponent does your team will be in trouble, you head the back of your opponent's head. One of two things happens: either you do enough to put him off and your opponent misdirects his header under the pressure, or you, him or both hit the deck holding your heads, in which case the game will be stopped for a head injury.

All perfectly within the laws of cheating, and something that you'll probably need to do some time in your career at a crucial moment in a game, but you never, ever practise it. It's like diving. The amount of people who ask me if we practise diving ... I mean, I ask you. If you feel a clip on your heel or a tug of the shirt, especially in the box, you fall over. How hard can it be?

But here was this centre-half actually practising heading the back of somebody's head for the next half-hour. I don't think that manager has a job right now; it's no surprise to me.

COULD I BE AN AGENT?

One way you can still earn a huge amount of money from football, after your playing days are numbered, is by becoming an agent, but it certainly isn't as easy as most players who move into it like to think. There's a lot of hard work involved, and a lot of baby-sitting. I know because I demand all that from my agent. And the competition is fierce: four big companies that dominate the industry, about 20 independent agents that each represent between 10 and 25 players (not all Premier League), and beneath them somewhere between 300 and 500 small fry. Some of these are doing a decent job, some are clueless and most are shysters. It is not uncommon for agents to receive bullets in the post after poaching players – not from fans but from other agents and their heavies.

I phoned an agent friend of mine, who is always good for a bit of information, as well as being a solid sounding board.

"What could you do for a player?" he asked.

"Well, I know what figures to ask for," I replied.

"Look," he said. "I'm not telling you not to become an agent but I know you – you haven't got the patience to build up an agency on your own. You'd be much better working in reverse as a director of football and doing deals that way round. You already know your budget and what you have to work with, and you work out a bonus with the club based on the money you have saved them in transfer fees and wages at the end of every year. That's much easier. Have you still got the offer of director of football?"

"Yes," I said.

"Take it, then. It's guaranteed wages and you could still play. It's a great opportunity."

"Yeah," I said. "But it's not going to make me rich, is it?"

There was silence on the line for a few seconds before the agent broke it. "Well, what about this, then? You become a front of sorts for an agent and bring him players and take a commission on each one who signs with him. Better yet, take a commission on all future deals for that player. Agents need footballers and footballers don't want to sign with ex-players, I'm afraid."

"Why not?" I asked.

"Think about it," he said. "Why would you choose to be represented by somebody who needed his own agent throughout his entire career? It's ridiculous."

I laughed. "I never thought of it like that."

Typical agent that he is, he had seen that I was cracking and gone for the jugular.

"And don't forget all the tricks of the trade," he said. "Depending on what type of player you're trying to sign, you need to be aware of what floats their boat. I've had a lot of success taking players to fancy restaurants and bars that they've never been in before and booking the table in their name. That makes them feel very important."

We have done our first deal together and, to be honest, I think this method has legs.

THERE'S ALWAYS GOLF

If none of this works out, I guess I'll be spending more time on the golf course. I used to despise the game, but I came to enjoy it after realising that you don't have to play it seriously: golf is all about who you are playing with, not the score you end up with. I remember playing with the captain of one of my old teams, who used to cheat terribly. If his ball went into the rough, he'd discreetly kick it out. I hated that. Now if my ball lands in the rough I just tell everyone I'm moving it to the fairway. You think I'm paying thousands of pounds for membership to stand in long grass and hack at a little white ball? No chance. I want to take my shots from where the pros take theirs.

Thankfully, where I live golf is a big deal and there are lots of nice courses. The waiting lists are all a year or more, but I solved that problem by giving a course manager and his son two season tickets for a club that I used to play for.

I'd be lying if I said I was welcomed with opened arms, though. On my first outing, a group of gentlemen who had been playing there for a hundred years complained that I wasn't wearing a collar in the clubhouse. This club didn't let women in until about 10 years ago, which tells you all you need to know about the men who play here, so I decided I wasn't going to take any shit from them. When a young Polish gentleman came to tell me that I would have to leave, I refused. We had a long debate about tradition, which I think I was able to demonstrate meant fuck-all in this instance, and he went to find his manager.

The manager came in and immediately thanked me again for the season tickets. He asked me if I knew the gentlemen who had complained about me, and explained that they were all from the club I used to play for – wealthy local business-men who had at some point held board positions there. I went over and shook all their hands, and a couple of them tried to make out that they had not complained, because they wanted autographs for their children. I signed, because that's what you do. From that moment on, wearing a collar in the clubhouse became optional.

I'd find it harder to fit in with the golfing culture else-where, however. My friend who used to play for one of the Old Firm once had a truly bizarre experience in South Africa. I'll let him tell the story.

"We were out there on a tour. I didn't want to go but I'd never been before, and I didn't have any choice anyway. A couple of the lads threatened to boycott it and were told that the fine would be two weeks' wages. They were furious but everyone turned up at the airport.

"By the time we got to South Africa we were exhausted and no good to train, so the manager said to take the day off and we'd start training proper the following day. The hotel was decent and you don't have to wander too far in South Africa before a member of staff tries to steer you towards a restaurant that their mate owns, or a club. On this occasion it was a golf course.

"We took a minibus down and went to the clubhouse to hire the equipment that we needed. We managed to get everyone into a slot and decided to play two lots of four-ball; each man put a grand in, so the pot was decent. We got a few buggies sorted out and went to pay for everything, at which point the woman behind the clubhouse bar said, 'Don't you want a jamhead? I notice none of you have ordered one.'

"I had no idea what she was talking about, but being Scottish and thinking that whatever it was would cost me money, I said no. But she was really insistent: 'Are you sure? Everybody has a jamhead.'

"I thought it must be a different type of club that they have out here because of the rough surrounding the course, but I couldn't think what it might be like – maybe a kind of rescue club. We didn't need any of that because if I lost a ball I wouldn't be spending any time trying to find it. So I told her we'd be fine because it was so hot we'd probably only do a few holes anyway. 'That's probably all you'll manage without a jamhead,' she said.

"We drove around to the first hole and got out of our buggies. The first hole had a magnificent-looking tree line with a beautifully kept fairway. It really made you want to play golf. But the flies and mosquitos were unbelievable – they were so bad that you found yourself spitting them out of your mouth every now and again. They were everywhere. I hit a quick shot and got back into the buggy, where the net curtains that were hanging down over the sides now made sense. We got to the third hole and caught up with a group in front of us; they offered to let us play through and we accepted. As we drove up the fairway, we could see one of their party looking for his ball and we jumped out of our buggies to help.

"The undergrowth in the trees was thick but there were hardly any flies, which I only thought was strange because it was so apparent that they had stopped buzzing around us. Just then there was a voice behind us: 'Sir, we ought to take a new ball because we're holding up the play.' I turned around to see a black fella standing there, surrounded by flies that had clearly been attracted to him by the huge smearing of jam on top of his shaven head. It was one of those things that instinctively forces a double take. So that was a jamhead!

"And as we drove around the course we saw jamheads everywhere, and they were all black men. I spoke to the guy looking for his ball; he was a white man from South Africa and didn't see any problem with a black man following him around with a load of jam on his head. 'He's just like a caddie,' said the man, 'except he keeps the flies away as well. They get well tipped at the end of the round.' Right. That makes it OK, then."

My own experiences of playing golf in foreign climes have rarely turned out any better. During what has become an infamous tour of America – a tour that has been referred to as "the best stag do I've ever been on" by a member of that squad that I still speak to – we took an afternoon off from the lash to play golf. The course was around the corner from our hotel but it was so hot that the four of us who were stupid enough to play in 100-degree heat took a cab all of 700 yards to the clubhouse entrance.

The course itself was a good one, like a links course almost surrounded by sea and swamp. I'm not a fan of America as a rule but this place was beautiful and the people were very friendly. About 10 holes into the round (and 10 beers, supplied by an all-too-frequent golf buggy that seemed to serve nothing but ice-cold Budweiser), I finally found some form. On the back nine I hit a rare but still glorious second shot with a 7 iron that flew straight down the middle of the fairway, before taking a favourable bounce to the left and running on to the green and past the flag. Although I then lost sight of it, I still felt smug.

We drove our buggies towards the green, and only then did I realise that the hole was elevated by a few feet, with the back half sloping towards a lake that lapped the edge of the green. I jumped out of the buggy, expecting the worst, and was relieved to see that the efforts of my previous shot hadn't been in vain. There was my ball with about an inch of grass between it and the water. I was determined to salvage my good shot and rescue a par; I even had delusions of chipping in for an unexpected birdie. To do that, though, I'd have to improvise, so I took my shoes and socks off and addressed the ball with my pitching wedge. I was only a few inches into the water but there's nothing worse than wet shoes and socks, plus I now had the perfect angle to chip back up the drop-away and towards the pin, for what would surely be the most impressive display of matchplay golf seen in these parts in recent memory.

I took a couple of practice swings and repositioned my feet several times before drawing the club back. This was going to be a historic moment, but just as the club reached the apex of the swing my moment in golfing folklore was halted by a startled team-mate looking past me and screaming, "What the fuck is that?"

I turned my head just in time to see two eyes and a long leathery nose rising out of the water. I absolutely shat myself, leapt on to the green and ran up the hill. I looked back just in time to see an alligator lower itself back into the water and, with a swipe of its tail, swim back out into the middle of the lake, where it sat peering back at us. I used to have a picture of it on my phone, but after a disastrous game I first smashed my mobile, and then threw it off a cliff.

Still, my place in sporting history was secured, even if it wasn't for the reason that I expected as I lined up that chip shot. Every now and again I get messages from a couple of the players who were there with me; one of them never tires of sending me pictures of the crocodile from Peter Pan. The tosser.

Could I spend the rest of my life like this, with or without the crocodiles? No way. Many of the things that people wait a lifetime to do more of, I have already been doing for 10 years. But I am not looking to take it easy; I am looking for a cause. Also, as I may have pointed out already, I can't afford to play golf all day.

PART THREE
THE ELEPHANTS
IN THE ROOM

The human cost of the beautiful game

WHERE WILL IT ALL END?

Years ago, heart monitors were the bleeding edge of scientific innovation as far as football was concerned. The beautiful game was, and maybe still is, far behind many American sports when it comes to using statistical analysis to improve individual performance, although the gap has narrowed considerably thanks to the surplus cash that most Premier League clubs can use to buy the latest technology.

Even though I no longer have the inclination to rigorously test the latest technological aids that our sports scientist lays his hands on, I get the hump when my younger teammates show the same blasé attitude, as this area of football is important to most players and can make a huge difference to both their ability and their attitude. I am a player of advancing years and have decided that I can't – or won't – be helped any more, but that doesn't mean I have no interest in sports technology.

In fact, I have become far more interested in this aspect of the game as I've got older. And that is because a growing amount of technology is finding its way into the game from all quarters, whether it was initially developed for the military or to help the physically challenged. Providing I don't have to be the guinea pig, I am prepared to be dazzled.

Last season I went to St George's Park in Burton, home to the FA's new 350-acre National Football Centre. On the day I went, the country had just experienced torrential downpours and there was flooding on the railways, all of which meant I turned up three hours late and missed Sepp Blatter, who had been shown around that morning. That was probably a good thing for both of us, however. I detest that man and have vowed that if we are introduced to one another, I will turn my back on him. I had always dreamed that it would be at Wembley in a big game, but our schedules never seemed to match. That has always been a major regret.

As you drive down a snaking road, past a few of the pitches and what I'm told will be a landing strip for light planes, an impressive building appears in the distance. The entrance to the facility is pretty imposing, with a wall of shirts either side of an awkwardly placed reception desk that backs on to a staircase. That's the first moment that you think that perhaps the FA held a competition to design the place and it was won by a chap who had cobbled something together in his lunch hour.

I am there to test some of the "state of the art" equipment, and God knows there's enough of it. Clearly no expense has been spared, but that's the problem: it appears as if people had been running around thinking, "We can have anything we like," rather than, "Do we actually need all this?" That said, some of the kit is fantastic. A big problem for physios is devising effective rehab programmes for players who are struggling to "load-bear": for example, somebody recovering from a cruciate ligament operation can't run too hard or lift too many heavy weights to build the muscle up, for fear that he will damage it again. Some clever spark has thought about that and given us the "anti-gravity treadmill" – a running platform that inflates around your lower body to reduce your weight by up to 80 per cent. This means you can still get a workout while keeping your rehabilitation as functional and specific as possible: it is perfect for those of us with injuries such as rolled ankles and, of course, cruciates.

The centre even has access to software that can predict injuries before they develop, and slow-motion cameras to see how you distribute weight and determine which parts of your body are susceptible to injury. One injury that it is hoped this technology can really benefit is Achilles' heel damage.

After watching everybody else test the equipment I make my way to the pool area, where another version of the anti-gravity treadmill exists in the form of a small pool, the floor of which can be lowered and spun exactly like a tread-mill, with underwater cameras to check on a player's running motion. It lends itself very well to hours of fun pretending to be Michael Jackson rising up out of the floor. There is a larger version at the other end, with a hot tub encircled by a cold plunge pool for hot and cold "contrast bathing".

I've soon had enough and go to find our sports scientist, who's in the gym.

"Some place, isn't it, mate?" I say.

"You think so?" he replies.

"What's wrong with it?" I ask

"It's shocking, mate. Nothing flows, you have to walk across corridors, there's frosted glass everywhere, which means you can't see through to keep an eye on the players. How are the physios supposed to check on the players from the treatment room when the gym is down the other end of the corridor? How can they make sure you're doing the work right? Look at the weights room – do you want to look over the indoor pitch while you're injured? It's demoralising."

"I didn't think of it like that," I tell him.

"Do you know who has designed this?" he asks

He has me hook, line and sinker. "No," I say. "A big name, was it?"

"An architect" he replies.

And he's bang on. Nothing makes any sense. The rooms are all over the place, and it's ridiculous that the physios can't keep an eye on the players doing their rehab work while they are treating others. In the Premier League and most of the Championship, medical facilities are always set up with that in mind.

In the gym room I find a guy sitting in a little office. He's not a physio: he's there to show people how to use the equipment. When I knock on his door he's surfing YouTube because I'm the only player around.

"Some place, this," I say.

"Yeah," he replies. "It would be good if somebody actually used it."

Believe me, I don't want to bash the FA over the head; I've come to realise that if we want to move ourselves further down the road as a footballing nation then we should all pitch in. But, my God, they really don't help themselves sometimes.

There is no doubt that the FA has put in place a building with great facilities. I keep hearing that the pitches are no good, but in fairness pitches can take a few years of regular use to get up to par. The top pitch is an exact replica of the hallowed Wembley turf – same dimensions, same grass, same curvature, same goals and nets, same everything. There is even a little stadium around it for the watching media and, no doubt, "friends of Uefa and Sepp". It was never going to be perfect but at least now we have a facility that is the equal of anything in the world. Whether that is a good thing is up for debate.

Something that sticks in my mind is an interview with members of the great West Indian cricket sides of the 1970s and 80s, in particular something that the legendary Viv Richards said. When he was growing up, he and his friends didn't have any proper equipment so they played cricket on the beach with baby coconuts and the thick part of a palm leaf as a bat. As a result they became extremely adept at judging the bounce of the oval coconuts, and very good at hitting them because the stalk of the palm leaf was only two or three inches wide. Their reactions were extraordinary and stayed with them right through their cricket careers. But once that generation of West Indian cricketers became successful in test matches and one-day internationals, the money began to arrive, and with it brand-new indoor facilities and state-of-the-art equipment for the next generation. The result? The standard dipped dramatically. It isn't enough to simply pass success off as "a golden generation", because there is always a reason for peaks and troughs.

My good friend Phil Taylor, the legendary darts player and winner of 15 world titles, told me that he practises on a board half the size of a regular dart board to improve his accuracy. Once when I played against him he even showed me a training exercise where he covers the board with a sheet of paper so he can't see any of the numbers and carries on throwing. His first two throws in that game were 140 and he was pissed off not to hit 180 – it was ridiculous. As a side note, when we played for real he was only allowed to use one dart to my three and he duly lost thanks to a memorable double 14 . Thanks, everybody. The other 15 games, however, didn't go quite so well for me.

Back to football. When Arsène Wenger came to the UK he stopped all the Arsenal youth teams from playing on full-sized pitches and reduced the number of players, before asking them to play across the pitch instead. That meant that each kid had more touches of the ball at a higher tempo and improved twice as fast. And what about the wealth of ridiculously talented Brazilian players who grow up playing Futsal, a five-a-side game with a slightly heavier ball that naturally stays on the ground, so that the kids have more touches with their feet while moving it more quickly? At St George's Park we apparently now have Futsal, but how many years did it take us to catch on? It is proven – we know it works. My own silly little example is that when my mates in the street were playing with a full-sized ball and barely able to kick it over 10 feet, I would practise against my garage with a tennis ball for hours. And I made it. OK, I'm not Lionel Messi, but I made it nonetheless. For me, less can definitely mean more.

Whatever the future of the England team, something needs to change today to give them any chance of winning tomorrow; this is the approach the FA has chosen, so we may as well get behind it. In terms of investment in facilities, grassroots and coaching the FA is probably doing all it can, which is not to say that there aren't ideas out there that will come along and improve football further. This area of our game is seeing a huge amount of investment at the top level. As a result, some very exciting things are beginning to emerge that, if successful, will change the landscape of football far beyond the borders of our country.

• • •

A good pal of mine works in partnership with one of the biggest clubs in the world and is one of those guys who becomes more excited as he tells you about the things that he's working on. I've known him for a long time and each time I talk to him he waxes lyrical about the next greatest thing to come into football, and how it is going to change the game as we know it. I met up with him at a charity night at a London hotel: he was as enthusiastic about his work as ever, and particularly about a device that he and his team had been working on with a technology company on the continent. I took the opportunity to ask him a bit about it.

"We have been interested for a long time in how to get information to players on the pitch," he told me. "You know what it's like: how many times has a manager shouted at you and you simply can't hear them? Our players complain sometimes that they have missed a key instruction because of the noise levels, and sometimes it costs them a goal or a chance. So what if you could have the information passed to you directly from the touchline? For me, the manager shouldn't even be on the touchline – he should be up in the stand with a team of people monitoring the game with every stat available to him, similar to American Football. He should be getting information from his team minute by minute and making his decisions with the information available rather than gut instinct. From up in the stand you can see everything; from the touchline all you see is one level – it's hard to see the spaces and the opportunities.

"One of the biggest problems we heard about from the manager of the club was that it was hard to get messages to the players because of the noise, so we developed and trialled something similar to Google Glass, which is a piece of eyewear that shows the user information in the corner of their eye on what is happening around them. It took a long time to develop, and one of the problems, ridiculously enough, was getting the font the right size so that the players' ball control wasn't compromised. Eventually we came up with a scrolling system rather than a small list of information; the code we use is receptive to eye movement and the glasses can be turned off with a double wink, so if a player is taking a penalty and wants to concentrate for a second he just has to double wink and the information will stop scrolling. This is the first step on the ladder of technology that works by simply having to think about a task. We're still not there yet, but we believe that we are very close to developing a system that can operate through a contact lens via a separate receiver somewhere else on the body."

"How big is the bloody receiver?" I asked.

"Well, that's the thing. It's still too big but it's only a matter of time before we get it down to a flexible, stick-on, Post-it-sized receiver that we strap around your chest."

"It sounds amazing, mate," I said. "What sort of information are you so keen to get to the players?"

"This is where it gets really exciting. We are opening up our stats department to our entire fanbase. The point of stats is to have as many as possible and the only way to do that is to have as many people contributing as possible. So if you have a stadium of 60,000 people, then why not get them contributing as well? We ran schemes at local tech companies and universities asking for fans of our club to contribute and the results were pretty unbelievable.

"One of our fans developed a pretty cool app that turns your phone into a heat-seeking camera. That means that he can sit in his corner of the stadium, hold his phone up and the app will show the heat of the players as they run around in real time. And that means that if we sync his app to the laptops of our staff members, who each monitor their individual player, they will be able to check if the player that they are responsible for is overheating, say, or not working hard enough. Once we build up the data over a few months we'll be able to see a pattern that may help us to see if a player is coming down with the flu, especially if he is hotter than he was the week before but the temperature on the day is lower.

"And that's just one app: we have people who have developed directional apps that show where players are running or passing, and not just for the home team either. If we can monitor what a particular player on the away team is doing then we can get that information to our players on the pitch. We can spot a game plan within the first minute, instead of waiting 10 minutes to see how the game pans out, then we can send a message to our players' lenses saying, 'This player is trying to hit or run into this area continually,' or, 'There is space in this area because the fullback isn't tracking runners.' And we can send this message out in any language, at any moment. Once we have these apps developed we will stop sending scouts to watch the opposition, we'll simply send 10 ordinary people to every away ground and capture the data from the game.

"The other advantage is that we can monitor the heart rates of the players, their sweat levels and how much liquid they are losing and how quickly their muscles use energy, all from the apps that have been developed. We can then tell a player to come to the side to get a drink way before his brain tells him he needs one; as you know, if you feel thirsty you're already dehydrated and a player who is dehydrated by only 1 per cent will see his performance reduced by 10 per cent. If you have 11 players who are all dehydrated by 1 per cent, your team ends up carrying a player. That's when it starts to make a big difference. We used to do this test by taking blood before training, but now we can do it in real time. That's the whole idea behind this – spotting a situation or a problem instantly, or even before it's happened, finding the solution and instructing the player as quickly as possible. That's the future. It will be science and technology that make the difference for the next superpower of football."

"It sounds phenomenal," I said. "Very clever, to the point that it must sail close to the edge where ethics are concerned."

"It's about winning, isn't it?" he said.

"That's what Lance Armstrong used to say," I pointed out.

"No, come on. This isn't the same as banned drugs – this is getting information to players in the digital age. What's the difference between this and players passing notes on to the pitch?" he asked.

"Good point," I said. "I don't know, but it just feels like it's underhand in some way."

"That's because you've never seen this before. It's brand new, and we're disrupting a game that, barring a few changes to the rules, has been played in the same way for 150 years. So anything new is going to look suspicious, but this is cutting edge and we'll sell it on the basis that it prevents injury by warning players that they are tired and dehydrated."

"So you *do* think it's cheating?" I joked.

"No, absolutely not," he said. "Every product has to be sold on something and it may as well be that, because we have to take into account the commercial potential, too. If we tie up with a major sports manufacturer when we're ready, this will become a huge commercial business. Forget all those heart rate monitors that people wear – when they go for a jog or to the gym they'll put their password in and pull down their entire training programme and even their personal bests."

"I agree, mate, it could be mega. It's like something the military use that then comes into the mainstream, like sat nav. So what's the plan now? When will it be ready?"

"Well, I think we're a couple of years away, then we'll have to do the required testing, similar to the years it took with goal line technology. But you may not see it: this is the type of product that a big tech firm will buy from us and shelve until the market is ready for it. So the question will be, can we afford to hang on to it or will the club ultimately decide to sell it on?"

Personally, I think it's genius and I've no doubt that it could change the game. Whether the game is ready for it, and I include the players in that, is another question. I'm inclined to agree with my friend: the likelihood of us seeing this in use in football is slim, not because it isn't a brilliant concept and product but because it is so valuable to other industries.

The future of this technology is to send players messages, pictures and video that enable them to see their own game in real time and adjust accordingly. As my friend explained, "A good example of that will be if we concede a penalty kick or find ourselves involved in a penalty shoot-out. We can actually send historical kicks taken by the penalty-taker that our keeper is standing in front of straight into our keeper's field of vision so that he can best determine which way to dive. If he stands on the goal line while the team are getting ready to take the kick, it will actually appear as if that player is taking an old penalty against him, so he'll be able to see body shape, the way he runs up and, ultimately where he is most likely to put the ball."

"But you're still going to need players who can cope with that level of information as well as play football at the same time," I said.

"Absolutely right," said my mate. "We're about 20 steps ahead of you. The players that we now take in at youth team level undergo a huge amount of testing themselves. The latest is bone testing, which means that we are able to determine what their physical attributes will be 10 or even 20 years down the line. That technology has been around for years, but nobody has ever thought to apply it to football players before. We can now find a really young kid who would otherwise have been lost to basketball, rugby or athletics and bring him into our youth team even if he can't kick a ball, because we know that years down the line he'll be 6ft 5in with a chance of becoming our number one goalkeeper and a valuable asset."

I have heard about this approach before, and to me, at least, it is interesting that my friend's club is not the only one thinking this way. I once wrote a column on the future of goalkeeping in which I quoted another friend of mine at a top-four club who said they didn't even consider goalkeepers now unless they knew they were going to be at least 6ft 2in. Crucially, they didn't care whether or not their recruits showed any aptitude as a goalkeeper because they felt they'd be able to develop them into the finished article.

"And these days bone testing has evolved so that we can now tell so much more physiologically about a player," continued my friend. "We can determine the size of a player's glute and hamstring muscles and the flexibility in their ligaments years down the line, which means we can work out roughly how fast they are going to be. It isn't an exact science like bone testing but it's crucial information for us. If we add this information to the neural technology that we now have, we can build up a really good picture of a kid's reaction times, his speed, his will to win and, of course, his physical stature. You watch: not too long from now there will be periodic testing on kids in schools by big football clubs. And the clubs won't be paying off parents any more to secure the services of their son: they'll be paying off the schools."

I remain very good friends with one of my old club doctors, who sits on the boards of a number of research institutions that are at the forefront of mental health and understanding neural behaviour.

"You can only be so fit," he told me. "You'll get the odd freakishly fit person, of course, but essentially all the players at the top level are going to be as fit as each other, and that means that more and more clubs are going to turn to sports science and specialised areas such as neural behaviour to gain an advantage.

"In the last few years there has been a tremendous leap forward in understanding the brain. In America the Obama administration has just announced a multi-million-dollar plan to map it. It is being sold as a chance to help people with neural disorders such as Parkinson's disease but it's more likely to have a military agenda to it.

"A big thing for us is neural behaviour. Specifically, we want to study the parts of the brain that deal with reaction times and decision-making. And we can do this now, thanks mainly to MRI scans that allow us to monitor brain activity in volunteers who are conscious and responding to a set of instructions. For example, we can give the subject a red ball and a blue ball and ask them to squeeze one or the other as soon as we tell them which. The quicker the part of the brain lights up that deals with reaction times, the faster that player is likely to be at making the right decision on the pitch. Providing he squeezes the right-coloured ball, of course. But even if he squeezes the wrong ball first, we can measure the time between the wrong decision and the right decision when he then squeezes the correct ball. That is also a reaction time that is important to us, because everyone is going to make a mistake from time to time."

And this is going on right now. Big clubs are beginning to screen their young recruits to help determine the potential of every player. If my friend is right and large clubs begin to subsidise schools in order to screen their best athletic talent, who will ultimately benefit? This could be the answer for the England team; this could be the chance to take a giant leap forward and possibly even steal a march on our rivals. But I'll bet you one thing: the FA don't even know about it.

THE PASTOR V THE PHYSICIST

Years ago, I played for a club that had a pastor as its designated sports psychologist. He was a nice guy but we used to have some fantastic ding-dongs. I'd load up on YouTube clips of Richard Dawkins and come in on a match day armed with ammunition to throw at him. "Do you really think that the earth is 5,000 years old?" I'd say, or: "Are we honestly saying that fossils were put there by the devil? You're an intelligent man: intelligent men admit when they are wrong." He gave as good as he got and took it all in good spirits. Years before I met him I was a serious atheist ... until some bright spark told me that by saying you're an atheist you are almost admitting that there is something up there to rebel against. The truth is that nobody knows what's out there or where to look. Are we saying that there is no God? Well, we can't prove that one way or the other.

Many years ago now, when I was just starting out in this game, I played for a non-league club. It is a club that I still go back to regularly. I've sponsored them, filled in as a part-time groundsman, brought teams to play there and played in charity matches (round of applause, please). I loved playing for that club: it was an amazing grounding and I had a manager who was a born winner. He helped to teach me the importance of winning, in fact, alongside a crazy foreign goalkeeper that I used to play with. He made the game feel like a war whose outcome would decide the fate of millions.

That club was fantastic for me because I was still finding my feet, both as a semi-professional footballer and as a man. I was so green, so naive, but I did have a determination not to be the worst player on the pitch. Because of that I was often one of the best, and with the help of my manager and a few of the senior players I became a very good player at that level. I liked the non-league scene: some of the things you hear people shout from the sideline are hilarious. Once an opposition manager jumped out of the dugout looking as if he was about to launch into a full-scale tirade at his centre half, only to shout, "Tone! Tone! Are you wearing fucking boxer shorts again? What have I told ya? Don't wear boxers – they make your knackers flap about," before calmly sitting back down.

The club is run by a committee whose members seem to have been there for a hundred years. And I never tire of giving them a bit of stick. I'll say, "I don't get it, John. When I was a kid down here, you were an old man; now I'm old and you're still an old man," and John will reply, "You're still a clever sod, though, aren't ya? No wonder your last club got rid of ya. Now give me your money for the golden goal – you haven't been down for a while, so £20 should do it."

That's what I love about these guys – they live and breathe the club. There was never any danger that any of them would blow smoke up my arse when I made it to the Premier League, and the lure of the tickets that I offered them was never able to trump a windswept, piss-soaked wooden stand in the back of beyond where they could watch their team play at a standard just below Conference level. But you should have seen them when I turned professional – I can't emphasise enough how happy they were for me.

My success also reassured them that they were doing the right things. I was the first player from that club to make it, and since I turned pro a steady stream of young and hungry players has been flowing out into the professional ranks.

Sadly, though, time refuses to stand still and we have lost a few very dear friends in the last few seasons – people who had been at the club for 30, 40 or 50 years in one capacity or another. Last year, my best friend lost his father, a committee member who had held various roles at the club and done as much as anybody to push it forward. It was a blow for everybody, particularly as we'd lost another stalwart of the club only a few months before. As usual, it was standing room only at the crematorium and when I arrived the queue to get in was already extending into the car park. I joined the end and made small talk with ex-managers and players, then I heard a whistle from the front of the queue. It was my mate and he was waving me towards him. This was awkward: I assumed that he wanted me to sit up front with the family, and as I walked past everybody I felt very uncomfortable, as if they thought I was getting special treatment – at a funeral, no less. When I got to the front of the line I could see the hearse but still nothing clicked.

"Listen," said my friend. "Would you mind being one of the pallbearers?"

I was honoured. "Of course not, mate."

"We're a bit early," he said, "so just have a chat with some people and come back over in about 40 minutes."

I had to call some friends to give them directions, so I went back to my car, as being seen on the phone at a funeral is very poor form. As I sank into the driver's seat, the button on my trousers flew off and hit the windscreen.

As is the usual process in moments as horrific as this, my initial bout of denial was followed by a swift cursing and denunciation of everything that God stands for. Eventually, I grudgingly accepted the reality of the situation and set about trying to come up with a plan. Unfortunately no plan could be found, and despite a brief – and fruitless – detour to a nearby pub on the offchance that they'd have a safety pin, I returned to the crematorium in a blind panic. The 40 minutes were up and my friend beckoned me to the front of the line to receive a crash course from the chief mourner in how to carry a coffin correctly. Unfortunately we didn't cover the thorny issue of how to keep one's trousers secure at the same time. By now I had broken out in a cold sweat.

"Put one hand here," said the chief mourner, "and the other arm across the shoulder of your mate next to you. We'll start off on the left foot. Ready?"

"Right." I thought. "Wherever Ted is, he must be absolutely pissing himself right now, so we may as well both go out in style."

The mourners took their seats and the place was absolutely packed. I put my arm across the shoulder of another ex-player from the club and began to step in time down the runway, left foot first. Almost as soon as I did, my trousers slipped an inch, then another. I tried to walk bow-legged so they wouldn't slip any lower than my hips, but I began to catch the foot of the man in front of me. The coffin was coming in sideways; I was waiting for the fire crews and accident investigators to appear along the sides of the aisle. It was going to be spectacular. I took another few steps and the trousers kept going, to the point where my Calvin Kleins put in an appearance. Another few paces and I caught the foot of the man in front of me again; this time the coffin shook violently and lurched to the right. My trousers retreated by another inch. By this time my jacket was riding up my back, giving the accident investigators a clear view of the problem.

Finally we made it to the conveyor belt. I was at the back and could not wait to get the coffin down. By now my trousers were revealing more than they were concealing. There was no getting away from it – this was an awful day to be wearing fuchsia-coloured underwear.

The guys at the front lowered their end of the coffin, then let go, leaving me struggling to do my bit with one hand holding up my trousers and the other still around the shoulder of the man next to me. The coffin went down with a hefty bump and the noise reverberated around the crematorium, drowning out the music for a moment. A few seconds later the terror was over and it was safely on the conveyor belt, much to everyone's relief, particularly mine. I took a deep breath and tapped the top of the coffin before casually pulling my trousers up. I turned to see the mourners in tears and I was grateful that I'd managed to prevent a disaster on this sad day. But as I walked back down the aisle, I realised that they weren't sad – they were crying with laughter. The lads at the back of the room were practically on the floor. I hope you're happy, Ted.

Back at the club where the wake was being held, I told my two friends what had happened: they had been sitting at the front with their mother and had missed most of the action. They cracked up, as I knew they would. As everyone who had been at the funeral told me, Ted would have been looking down and absolutely pissing himself. And that, in a nutshell, is how a footballer who escaped a small town and made it to the big time never had a prayer of forgetting his roots. I love these people.

• • •

My laptop was open but I hadn't so much as glanced at it since switching it on. I hadn't even noticed the table changing hands. When I'd walked into the coffee shop there had been a very promising brunette that I'd taken for a student sitting there. She'd been sipping a frothy latte when I last looked but at some point during the last 10 minutes she'd taken the decision to get on with her life. Her replacement was a tall, conservatively dressed, middle-aged man.

I returned to doing nothing, gazing through the window towards the end of the street where a seemingly endless stream of students were emerging in a way that suggested they didn't exist until the very moment that I laid eyes on them. The man next to me was people-watching too, but he introduced an extra dimension by commentating as people ran out in front of a car – "Woah, steady!" – or offering a merry "After you!" as strangers converged on a pavement and blocked each other's paths. There was no getting away from it: all the signs pointed to a man spoiling for small talk.

Closing my laptop, I made the mistake of taking a final look through the window. It proved fatal.

"You look lost," said the man.

Had I been taking my medication as I was supposed to, I could have batted him away and been down the road before the waitress even had a chance to clear my table, but my quick wit had flicked into screensaver mode weeks earlier.

Since that time Mr T, as we'll call him, has become a great friend and instilled what has become a bit of an obsession with physics and, in particular, quantum mechanics. Most of my understanding of the subject is a couple of rungs below the Idiot's Guide to Quantum Mechanics entry level, while he is a professor working on some incredible experiments at Cern. Still, we get on famously

I love quantum mechanics: it's so strange that, on the surface at least, much of it appears to be impossible. But this strand of physics continues to pass all the tests that are thrown at it. Despite the black holes that persist in certain areas of the research, it remains the one part of my life that continues to offer me some kind of meaning whenever I revisit it. It makes me feel insignificant, but in a way that helps me to dispense with all the bullshit going on around me.

My interest was first piqued by a programme on Erwin Schrödinger, the great Austrian physicist and Nobel prize winner; his work is what helps me get through the mundane reality of life. The deeper I go, the less I understand and the more reassured I feel. That reassurance comes from something that Schrödinger described as "the wave function". In short, two particles can become so deeply linked that a measurement of one particle immediately influences the other. For example, if we know that each of a pair of entangled particles is either red or blue, and we want to determine the colour of each one, we need to make a measurement of one of the particles.

The mathematics that underpins quantum mechanics tells us that the instant we measure the particle and determine that it is blue, the other entangled particle will turn to red. This is called "collapsing the wave function". And this happens no matter whereabouts in space the other entangled particle is. So even if the other entangled particle is 100 light years away, and despite the fact that we know that nothing can travel faster than light, the other entangled particle will still, instantly, turn to red. How is that possible? Nobody, not even Mr T, knows the answer.

It is thanks to Mr T that Schrödinger's Cat became entangled with this column about racism. Initially my idea was to have a black cat and a white cat as the lead-in, but it threw up so many problems that not even Mr T could resolve them.

SHADES OF GREY

First published 30 January 2013

I love Schrödinger's Cat. There are many versions of this famous paradox but here's my favourite.

We put a cat in a bunker with some unstable gunpowder that has a 50 per cent chance of exploding in the next minute and a 50 per cent chance of doing nothing. Until we look in the bunker, we don't know if the cat is dead or alive, but when we do look, sure enough – it is dead or alive.

If we repeat the experiment with enough cats and gunpowder, then half the time the cat will live and half the time it will die. But before we look, the cat is dead and alive; it is only the act of looking that forces nature's decision. For the cat's part, it will either see the gunpowder explode or not.

So the gunpowder explodes and the cat sees it explode or the gunpowder doesn't explode and the cat doesn't see it explode. The cat's reality becomes entangled with the outcome of the experiment and it is only our observation of the cat that forces nature to collapse into one reality.

Thank God – or physics – that football isn't as complicated. At least, it never used to be. The globalisation of our game means that domestic football in this country is now represented by players from all over the world who bring with them different faiths and cultural traits that entangle with our own.

Occasionally, some of these different cultures smash together with all manner of pundits, journalists and fans eager to give their interpretation of the results.

If I were to ask members of our youth team on a Monday morning whether anybody from the FA or the Premier League has ever spoken to them about racism, I would bet everything I hold dear to me that every single one of them would say no.

So one of two things happens: either players try too hard not to say something that could be construed as racist – and do. Or nobody says anything. And that is particularly scary.

The problem is that there is a lack of real education on the issue. Throwing T-shirts at players to wear before matches is not education.

Don't get me wrong. We all know what racism looks like in its crudest form, such as the disgraceful monkey gestures we've seen in the Premier League from some fans, or the throwing of bananas on to the pitch, as happened to the Brazilian left-back Roberto Carlos while playing in Russia.

What is required is a little education to fill in the grey areas. Take Alan Hansen, a former Liverpool player who is now a pundit on Match of the Day, who in 2011 described black players as "coloured". There but for the grace of God – or physics – go I. Because when I was growing up in the early 1980s, my father was at pains to point out that the correct term for a black person was "coloured".

I was told to call the man who lived on the end of our row "Indian", even though I am convinced that nobody had a clue where he was from. We certainly never used the P-word, even though at the time it could be heard on some of the nation's most popular TV shows.

Of course, nobody is going to tap you on the shoulder 10 or 20 years later with an update and, as we know, so much of what a person learns in childhood will shape their adult life. But that doesn't make it acceptable to plead generational or cultural ignorance.

It took an FA-led commission, whose report ran to 115 pages, to determine whether or not the Liverpool striker Luis Suárez had racially abused the Manchester United defender Patrice Evra in 2011. The commission had to consider that in Suárez's native Uruguay, the word "negro" is a widely used term with which black people greet one another. But, after all, Suárez is mixed race and playing his football in England.

Suárez was eventually banned for eight games and fined £40,000 due to a lack of video evidence.

Keep in mind that John Terry, the former England captain, was banned for four games, despite all the video evidence that was presented during his hearing on whether he had racially abused Anton Ferdinand, the QPR defender.

Perhaps the most lenient punishment of all came in December 2012, when Uefa imposed what Kick it Out chairman Lord Ouseley described as a "paltry" £65,000 fine on the Serbian FA after England's black players were racially abused during an Under-21s match in Kruševac.

The Professional Footballers' Association can occasionally be heard in the middle distance calling for tougher punishments. But its chief executive, Gordon Taylor, would do well to get in front of the players instead of the TV cameras he seems to prefer. In the absence of any leaders educating the next generation, we continue to see unsavoury episodes.

We are moving very quickly towards a state of extreme paranoia, where everybody is a racist until it's proven that they're not. Take the farce at Stamford Bridge last year, when Chelsea complained that referee Mark Clattenburg had called midfielder John Obi Mikel a "monkey".

When I phoned my friend at Chelsea, who was in the dressing room as things were kicking off, he told me that even the rest of the Chelsea players didn't believe Mikel and said as much to him.

But Mikel's claim was backed up by his Brazilian teammate Ramires, who, as my friend put it, "hardly speaks any English".

It is common knowledge that Clattenburg calls almost every player on the pitch by his nickname and, as my friend said: "We know in all likelihood that the ref has called him 'Mikey' but what can we do?" Premier League rules state that clubs have to make their complaint after the game, when tensions are obviously running high and people are emotional.

Again, as my friend said: "We didn't want to complain but we had to." Fair enough, but the fact the story made its way into the public domain almost before the players had left the stadium could have cost Clattenburg his career if the story hadn't been so unbelievable. Fortunately, he was later absolved.

You don't need me to tell you that a football changing room is a unique place to work in. We bend more rules than the Catholic church and each player will be pushed as close to their tolerance threshold as possible in an attempt to find the boundaries of acceptable mockery.

There are examples of this behaviour every single day. During the running sessions in which the fitness coach will tell you, "We're looking for winners," the person who crosses the line first will usually be abused based on a strong feature that they have – a person with a big nose might hear a fellow professional shout: "He won it by a nose!"

There are also individual players who have their own unique relationship with each other. I know a black player and a white player who go out of their way to deliver insult after insult about each other's race and personal appearance. They are strong characters, enjoy engaging each other on that level and treat their relationship, it seems to me, as a test of quick wit. It's worth pointing out that they do it only in front of the squad.

It's been like that at every club I've played for. I remember a ball getting stuck in a tree at one club and a black French player saying to an African player, "You climb this tree – you're a bigger monkey than me," before the pair of them fell about laughing.

Tackling racism should never be considered the job of one person or organisation. The task is too great and, if I may say, too diverse. Nobody seems to know what the right thing to say is any more; this prevents people from stepping forward to speak out.

Maybe quantum mechanics is easier, after all. In Schrödinger's book What Is Life? he talks about each individual's consciousness as being only a manifestation of a unitary consciousness that pervades the universe. His best-known work on wave mechanics, known as Schrödinger's Equation, goes some way to explaining the interconnectivity of the universe at a quantum level.

Think of Suárez and Evra as ocean waves, or tornadoes. At first glance, they appear to be two separate bodies, but they're not. That is simply the way we choose to perceive them. Waves and tornadoes are simply water and wind stirred up in different directions. The truth is that nothing is separate and everything is related. The colours that we see exist only in our own consciousness.

With thanks to Mr T, working at Cern.

• • •

"Philosophy and science are two different things and never the two should meet," said Mr T, when he eventually saw the finished article. I had been pretty pleased with the final column up until that point, but this latest review was tough to take, given that it came from the man who had inspired the article in the first place. At the very least he owed me an explanation.

"OK," I said. "What's wrong with it?"

"That bit at the end," said Mr T. "You're into the realm of philosophy. None of what you end that article with can be tested in a controlled way – it's all theory and speculation. You begin with a sound version of Schrödinger's Cat, which is fine – nobody disputes that the wave function collapses when we observe it because that is something that can be shown to be the case with the right experiments – but how are you going to prove that absolutely everything in the universe is connected?

"Well, I was going down the route of entangled particles, really, and scaling it up a bit," I said.

"That's fine," said Mr T. "You should have written about entangled particles, then."

"Hmmm ... Why don't you fuck off?" I ventured.

Mr T laughed. "Because according to that article, there's another one of you out there somewhere begging me to stay; so just this once I'm going to assume you're half right and listen to that other you."

• • •

Quantum mechanics is the only thing that has enabled me to put the phone down on people chasing me for money, or to turn a blind eye to the bottles that were thrown at me last season by the "fans" of my old club after a match at their ground. It enables to me to treat everything with less importance than I would otherwise.

I can remember vividly the first game after I really got into it: I was playing against West Ham United at Upton Park and the ball had gone out for a throw-in to my team. I ran off the pitch to retrieve it, to the usual hail of abuse. I looked up and saw these big, bald, middle-aged men looking down on me from little plastic chairs for which they'd probably over-paid. They seemed to vent in unison with a sort of slow and rhythmic, yet forceful, tirade of abuse. And I was picking up a football. I felt so sorry for them. I felt as if I knew some-thing that they didn't and it made me pity them immediately.

Since that moment, none of the peripheral shit that goes on around me every day has bothered me. I remember when HMRC came to see me at my house; halfway through our meeting the man who revels in delivering bad news on behalf of Her Majesty leaned forward and said, "You don't seem to be taking this as seriously as perhaps you ought to. You owe us more than a million pounds."

If there are no definitive explanations and answers to the fundamental questions of life, then anything is still possible. And that is an incredibly exciting place to be – it is literally what has kept me alive. The fact that there are no answers is, in fact, the answer.

THE AWFUL ROWING
TOWARD HAPPINESS

Last season, not for the first time since I became The Secret Footballer, I found myself writing about depression. It drove me crazy – I just couldn't get into the right frame of mind to describe it. I played all the songs that I used to have on a loop when the depression was at its worst, to try to stir the right – or wrong – emotions. The main one was Peter Gabriel's Mercy Street. It was based on the poem 45 Mercy Street, which started life as a play and ended up as the title of a book by Anne Sexton, a renowned poet who suffered from manic depression – or, as we would now call it, bipolar disorder.

Sexton's writing has been a huge influence in my life, and her 1975 work The Awful Rowing Toward God has been a perpetual source of inspiration. I never met her – she died before I was born – but I feel incredibly close to her. I can't explain that feeling, except to say that each time I read any part of that book it feels as though she is talking directly to me and about my life.

Anne Sexton was still alive when her publishers set a release date of March 1975 for her book, even though she had told them that she would not allow it to see the light of day until after her death. On 4 October 1974, she met her good friend Maxine Kumin, a fellow writer with whom she would share early versions of her work. During that lunch the two discussed the first drafts of The Awful Rowing. On returning home, Sexton put on her mother's old fur coat, removed all her rings and poured herself a glass of vodka before locking herself in her garage. She started the engine of her car and killed herself by carbon monoxide poisoning.

At one point I very nearly followed Anne Sexton down the rabbit hole and I still can't shake the morbid curiosity that lies deep within me, despite all the medication.

The column wasn't going well. I don't know whether it was because my medication had some kind of memory-erasing property that I wasn't told about, or I was simply in a state of permanent happiness. And that was always my reluctance in turning to drugs. It's difficult to tell who the real me is any more. In my attempt to find out and to write a column that I'd be happy to put my pseudonym to, I wandered down a familiar and dangerous path: I made the decision to stop taking my medication.

The problem was, I didn't know how long it would take for my artificially inflated serotonin levels to revert to their natural position – given how I felt before I went on the medication – somewhere south of bugger-all. And I couldn't ask the doctor who prescribed the drugs because I knew he'd talk me out of this risky decision. I didn't want that. I needed to find that dark place where the simple things of everyday life are as painful to contemplate as they are impossible to act on.

With my limited medical knowledge and an absurd amount of faith in Google, I came to the misinformed conclusion that if it takes the body several weeks to build up effective serotonin levels on a particular medication, it must take the same amount of time for them to reduce. As one of my old physios used to say after another unsuccessful self-diagnosis, a little bit of knowledge is a dangerous thing.

But I'd concluded, rightly or wrongly, that the only way to write the column was as a person who hadn't only been there but still was there, just like Anne Sexton when she wrote those agonising poems. I don't feel competitive with The Awful Rowing Toward God, but I do feel that I have something to live up to – if that's the right choice of words for this situation. Only somebody trapped at the bottom of the rabbit hole can offer a true account of depression, provided they can find it within themselves to put that account into words.

So I got a month's extension to my deadline and flushed the medication.

In the event, the changes were fairly swift. I began to experience signs that something wasn't quite right within 48 hours. I have missed taking medication before; I once left my washbag on the coach on the way back from an away game and it took the coach operator three days to get it back to me, by which time it had been on an outing to Blackpool.

The effects of being clean and not altogether that sober are strange, to say the least. I find that my vision is affected in a most peculiar way, as a tingling feeling shoots through my eyes at random moments in the day. And it is most inconvenient. I have had to "style it out" in a lot of difficult situations, the worst of which came when I had to suddenly grab the arm of an elderly man as I was crossing the road. It was ridiculous: here was this young(ish) man, an athlete no less, being escorted across the road by a pensioner. The worst part of the whole sorry episode came as I lunged to grab his arm: he looked up at me and said, "Thank you." Piss-taker.

When this happens, playing football is difficult. I have actually been on the ball when it has happened and I wasn't able to cover it up. I remember putting my foot on the ball when it was obvious to everybody watching that I should pass. I just couldn't co-ordinate myself. But at that point in my career, and with that particular club, I was receiving so much abuse that I could have walked off. Weeks later, I told my manager to take me off while the game was going on but he just looked at me and asked, "Are you injured?" I didn't know what to say; technically, I suppose I was.

Mirtazapine, the part of my medication that allows me to sleep at night, is so effective that it knocks me out within 20 minutes of my consuming it. The dose that I take is very strong and works by relaxing the muscles that have been on edge all day. Not too long ago, I took a double dose because my roommate and I had been out for dinner and I'd had Coke by the bucketload – the drink, that is. I'd followed that with a coffee, the upshot of which was that I was wide awake gone midnight. But at that hour my body tends to fail me: instead of the double dose making me drowsy, it just relaxed my muscles to the point that I couldn't speak properly because my tongue was hanging out of my mouth and my face wouldn't move. My roommate was crying with laughter and accused me of feigning a stroke for attention. But I digress.

Two weeks into my "clean and not so sober" project, I crashed spectacularly. I don't know why it came to me but I couldn't get Jefferson Airplane out of my head: when the shakes came, I remember hearing the opening bars of White Rabbit. Then the flashbacks began. I saw my father as he would have looked 25 years earlier. But the image I had of him was not one that I remembered ever seeing before. As the withdrawal went on, so the song became more persistent, but I wasn't capable of working out why I was even thinking about it. I just saw my father standing in our old house looking out of a window that took in a view that didn't belong there. But he was facing away from me and if I walked toward him the distance between us grew. I knew he had a message for me, but at that moment he wasn't ready to give it to me for some reason.

In his prime, my father was a handsome man, with jet-black hair and a natural golden tan. He was strong, too: he had the arms of a boxer and could be imposing when I ignored my mother's calls to come in for dinner or when I should have been concentrating on homework instead of playing football. And he had an eccentric streak, brought about by a desire to learn. He could berate his football team on the television while reciting a Shakespeare play for a course that he'd enrolled in at the local college; he had the brawn and skill to build many of the houses that surrounded our street, while retaining an interest in the stained glass that would eventually end up inside their sitting rooms. He was inspirational.

And as I watched him for the best part of 20 years, I came to believe that I could do anything with my life, whenever I wanted to do it. That belief often manifested itself in selfish and destructive behavior, but on the whole it resulted in bursts of creative energy.

I remember so much of my childhood. Although I gave my parents plenty of cause for concern, those were fantastic years, full of love and every advantage that my parents could afford. Above all, they passed on a level of wisdom that I'm now beginning to take advantage of. Because of all that, it didn't seem right that I couldn't place this image of my father looking out the window.

So here is the column. It took a ridiculous amount of sacrifice and stupidity to write it. Was it worth it? Probably not. It's just a column, after all.

DOWN THE RABBIT HOLE

First published 20 September 2012

"They fuck you up, your mum and dad." According to Larkin they do, anyway. The quote sticks in my head not least because, strangely, it was something that my dad used to say to me when I was about 13 years old before slapping a copy of the poet's 1974 book High Windows into my hand.

At the time, it was difficult to know what to think. On the one hand, it was an extremely steep learning curve, way beyond anything that I was capable of digesting; but on the other, it sowed a seed in my mind that has only just begun to germinate – that with the right influences and the right teachers, a person has the ability to do and say what they please.

If you're lucky (or not), you may even find an audience, if what you seek is fame and attention. I never wanted to be famous.

But things in our house were never quite how they first appeared. When I was still of Disney age, I remember being sat down to watch Alice in Wonderland. It was a surreal experience – of course it was. The story makes no sense and features a succession of nightmarish characters that could quite easily pass for somebody's version of hell. Then, one day, my father told me to watch it again: "Right, now listen to this song and tell me what you think Alice in Wonderland means."

The song was White Rabbit, by Jefferson Airplane, and I happen to be listening to it as I type this. The song seemed to finish with a thousand doors all swinging open in unison as the band's female singer, Grace Slick, belted out the line, "Feed your head, feed your head." And that's when I understood.

"Feed your head, feed your head" – it was an acid trip. Everybody works that out eventually, of course, but when you work it out at the age of 12, things are never quite the same again.

When it is obvious that all you want to do as a kid is play football, these interruptions are as curious as they are eccentric, but my outlook on life really began to change out of all recognition when I became a footballer. Until that point, I had been in search of some perspective to life – a meaning, if you like – and I felt that it wasn't far away.

I still continued to look for these little insights into life while having to live a very sterile existence as a sportsman. You can be the most successful footballer who ever graced the pitch, but you're never any closer to finding a meaning than somebody who has only played a handful of pub games. It doesn't matter how many medals you win.

The level of attention that a top-flight footballer pays to mundane things such as practice, hydration, rest and nutrition is extremely important if you are to maintain any success in the game. But it is also incredibly frustrating because it accounts for a lot of time that could be spent stimulating the mind.

After a while, the things that made me a great footballer hampered my life progress and I came to resent every one of them. This, in turn, led me down a very dark path.

It is a feeling that I still have to this day, although the edge has been taken off by the medication I now take. Football has only ever provided me with any great joy in the immediate aftermath of winning a game. When you win a game of football, it is a unique feeling. Winning says, "I'm better than you, and the lads that I play with are also better than you." It's a playground mentality, deep rooted in us all, that comes racing to the surface in the wake of a success.

But losing a football match is a terrible feeling. Worse, being responsible for that loss with a mistake feels as if the whole world is pointing at you and laughing while taking pot shots at your stomach.

Afterwards, you arrive home alone, with just your thoughts for company. That's when a player suffering from depression is extremely vulnerable. I know, because I went through it for nine tenths of my career. Everything about football, other than winning, feels like a grind. To me, at least.

I can recall being comprehensively beaten by Arsenal. That was when a little piece of my life fell apart. Until that moment, I had felt quite comfortable as a footballer in the Premier League; I never looked out of my depth and, if anything, I performed very well.

I watched the DVD of that match over and over again, trying to work out how the Arsenal players were doing what they did. It was like Brian Wilson listening to Sgt. Pepper on a loop. "How do they do this?" I asked myself. "How can I do it?" Once the game becomes complicated in your head, there is no way back.

I became even more withdrawn, to the point where I'd come in from training and sit on my own, staring at the wall. The TV wasn't on and the curtains were usually drawn.

I can't even remember if I had any thoughts about life. It was just an emptiness – a hopeless void that was only punctuated at certain points of the day by playing a game that I had come to hate. For me, that is the "spiral" effect that you sometimes hear sufferers of depression talk about.

Around the training ground, I became extremely volatile and would find myself in conflict with a different person nearly every day. It was all I could do to get through it. I just wanted to go home and stare at the wall again. The wall never answered back, you see.

At its worst, I drove to the training ground, took one look around at the familiarity and turned around. My brain had started to associate everything with unhappiness.

The silver BMW belonging to our striker, which was the first car I saw in the morning, now filled me with dread; the groundsman who used to grunt "Good morning" to me while having his morning fag became a figure of repetitive torture.

And then I'd walk through the changing room doors, only to be confronted by the usual banter regarding my shoes, my jeans or the fact that I was late.

The safety mechanism that prevented me from engaging in any violence in the split second after I arrived was to go straight through to the boot room and stay there for a couple of seconds before walking back in with my boots. Those few seconds were very important. They saved a lot of people from a lot of punches, me included.

In any football club, there are one or two players who live and breathe football. They have to be first even in the warm-up and, for me, they became my barometer whenever I came into training. The more these two pissed me off for no reason, the more susceptible I felt I was to blowing up. I hate warming up: it is without doubt one of the most tedious things in a footballer's career, particularly when you do the same warm-up day in and day out.

One day, I think I must have cracked – either that or I had a moment of clarity without realising it. "I don't want to do this any more," I thought to myself. "This must be one of the most pointless things that any person can do with their life." And with that, I walked out of the training ground and went home. I surfaced from my bedroom three days later. The crazy thing is that, when I went back to training, nobody said a word. Not the players, not the coaches and not the manager.

Years later, after I had become all but a recluse, my club doctor invited me into his office to talk about my moods. He took one look at me and asked: "How is your mental health?" That's when I knew that he'd busted me.

I told him everything that had happened to me in the last however many years, which didn't take as long as I'd thought because I hadn't done anything worth doing. I didn't go out and I didn't talk to anyone.

The levels that I'd sunk to are all too obvious if I look back at the first few months of my treatment. Below is an extract of a conversation that my club doctor was kind enough to pass on to me for this article. We think that this is probably about three months into my treatment.

Doctor: "Don't worry: you're not different to anyone else."

Me: "No, doc, you're wrong. I am different. I used to 'get' it but now I've lost it."

Doctor: "What did you 'get'?"

Me: "Everything, doc. I was close to understanding every-thing and now it's gone."

Doctor: "Do you mean football or something else?"

Me: "Something else."

Doctor: "Do you know what that is?"

Me: "Not any more."

Doctor: "OK, I think we should take your citalopram dosage up from 20mg to 40mg, just for a few weeks to see how we get on. I'd also like you to see a cognitive behavioural therapist as quickly as we can. Do you have anyone local who can escort you home today?"

Doctors only ever ask that when they are worried that you will throw yourself under a train.

For what felt like a split second after I upped my medication, I thought I was home. I immediately felt that I might be able to get back to what I was doing before football.

Alas, this turned out to be nothing more than a Proustian brush with a remembrance of things past. I remain convinced that there is something more to life but, although I got the treatment that I clearly needed, the answer has never felt so far away. Whatever that was, I am certain that I was on to it before this game got in the way. Football has seriously fucked me up.

• • •

So that's the column taken care of. But here I am, thanks to my Method approach to writing, deep in the rabbit hole once more.

When the depression hits this time, after another disastrous match, I'm so tired that I skip the meal my wife has left out for me. I tell myself that I shouldn't be feeling this bad. I can't even be bothered to get my toothbrush out of my washbag or pour myself a glass of water to take up. I never drink it, anyway: an entire reservoir must have given its life in pints of water that I take to bed and never drink. I turn the lights off in the kitchen and head up the stairs. They creak as I ascend and I become aware of the noise reverberating around the landing.

The child gate at the top of the stairs seems like a deliberately placed torture device and I fumble for the mechanism that unlocks it. It swings open, but closing it behind me is out of the question. I tell myself that my wife will notice it in the morning before she takes the little one out of bed and puts him down to run around.

My body is crying out to turn right towards our bedroom but something stronger pulls me to the left, where two doors are pulled to. I walk to the first one and nudge it open; the bottom of the door brushes the carpet and stops abruptly as the energy I have put into the gesture runs out. In the middle of the room is a bed whose Toy Story sheets cover a little boy with his knees pulled up to his chest. I can't bend down – my knees and back won't allow me to – and I stare at him for a minute before kissing my hand and tapping the top of his head with it. He immediately turns over to face the other side of the room and I decide to let him be. I close the door behind me and walk towards the second door, but as I put my hand out to open it I can hear what sounds like whispering.

It's pitch black and my brain is so tired that it can't work out which of my senses it should heighten. I stand at the door and pull myself together. One half of me is very aware that there is no blunt instrument to hand if whoever is on the other side of the door poses some sort of threat; the other half is thinking that I should have brought up that glass of water, as I'm suddenly very thirsty. I strain my ears and just make out a woman's voice.

It is my wife, singing White Rabbit quietly to the younger of our two sons.

The next morning I wake and slip downstairs. I walk into the kitchen and two little boys run up to me: "Daddy!" I kneel down and hug them; I smother them. "Lift us!" The older one always says that; I'm not quite sure what it is about being a few extra feet off the floor that is so exciting for little kids, but I don't argue. As I try to lift them, however, my body screams. It's as if one of my enemies – and there are many – is driving a chisel between my vertebrae.

"Come on, Daddy! Lift us!" I try again and somehow hoist them into the air. Their smiles widen, but now they're up they have no idea what to do. So we stand there for a moment and hug each other while the younger one sticks his finger up my nose, something he finds hilarious and revolting at the same time. He couples his laughter with a shudder that makes the rest of us of us crack up.

"I heard you singing to this one last night," I say to my wife, who is making me a coffee.

"When?"

"Last night," I repeat. "When I came up to bed I could hear you in his room singing to him. I didn't want to go in as it sounded as if you were trying to get him off to sleep."

"I stopped going into his room when he was about a year old. I didn't get up last night at all." She gives me a look somewhere between pity and anger. It's gone too far now – I've been losing it for the last few months and she's had enough.

I put the boys down and go back upstairs to where my phone is charging. Ignoring the text messages, emails and breaking news notifications, I open my contacts and tap in the name of the one man who can help me. But he isn't there. I delete the name and instead search for "Doc" but I already know what is about to happen. About 20 contacts flash up; it turns out that I have a doctor for every ailment. "Doc (knee specialist)", "Doc (groin specialist)", "Doc (back specialist)" ... it seems they are all specialists in one thing or another. When you meet them they tend to appear before you in full Savile Row regalia, with some sort of grandfather clock time-piece hanging off their wrist. Fortunes, they charge. One of my heroes, Kenneth Williams, summed up the situation: "I should think in the old days you were better off because nowadays they're all specialists. Everyone's becoming better and better at less and less, and eventually someone's going to become superb ... at nothing."

Eventually I narrow it down to three contacts, all down as "club doctor". I call the first of them: "The mobile you have called was last used seven years ago by somebody claiming to be a knee specialist, who now lives very nicely in that tax haven of the Turks and Caicos Islands." I try the next one: "This is the Vodafone voicemail service for 0789 ...

The person you are trying to reach did even better than the last specialist you rang, bought a very nice loft in New York and now spends his days becoming increasingly eccentric around Greenwich Village."

The last doc answers straight away. "Hello, my friend. How are you?" he says.

"Not good, doc," I say. "Not good at all. I've lost it."

"Where are you now?"

"At home."

"Stay there – I'll be there in an hour. Are you on your own?"

"No, the wife and kids are here," I say.

"Don't let them leave the house before I get there." And he rings off.

Fortunately, the doc was able to put right what I had fucked up, but it took many months. And once I got back to a point where I could function again, I had a very clear feeling that what I had been searching for didn't exist. The best that I can hope for is to find a way to survive the regularness of life.

Oh well.

I guess that not every story ends with the hero landing on his feet.

EPILOGUE

THE REAL MEANING
OF FOOTBALL

I always told myself that I wouldn't push my kids into sport. When playing football was making me feel like topping myself, I vowed that I'd keep them away from it altogether. But my older son is now at the point where he wants to try the things that he does in the back garden, like football, mini-golf and swingball tennis, with other kids. Near our house there is a flashy country club that caters for children whose parents drag them there kicking and screaming and dressed in all the gear, with every possible accessory. It is an extremely competitive environment and I get off on the fact that while we don't fit in because we don't come from money, most of the other members would love their children to be professional sportspeople, like me.

I sneer at these people – or at least I did – because the kids aren't playing for the enjoyment of it. They're playing for their parents, and all the flash kit in the world can't conceal the fact that they aren't about to pick up a tennis racket or a golf club and perform like Roger Federer or Tiger Woods, no matter how far their parents stick their tongues up the teacher's arse. They'll probably all grow into very successful adults – and maybe the competitive spirit that they pick up now will play a part in that – but it rather flies in the face of my fairly liberal approach to parenting. I'd like my own kids to be successful but I'd much rather they were happy.

However, it seems I have passed my own hunger to win down to my children. My older boy is still in the phase of smashing things if he loses at Connect Four, but if we can turn that frustration into a positive we might have something we can work with.

I tried him at golf, but that didn't go well. There was an unfortunate incident with a duck that wondered out of his flash lake and across the flash driving range, to catch a flash of my son's iron across his head on a follow-through swing. It was a distressing moment for all the kids who witnessed it, and we've since been branded "the duck killers".

Next I took him to the squash courts, because what kid doesn't like hitting a little ball as hard as he can wherever he likes? The problem is that a squash court is a sterile environment, and as soon as you introduce rules the fun goes out of the window and the boredom flies in. It was the same with tennis, where the ball rarely made two consecutive visits over the net. Don't even get me started on cricket. There was only one thing left to try, and I faced the uncomfortable truth that my son was going to have to have a go at football.

We took a trip to one of the big sports stores and he chose his first pair of boots. "I want the same as Daddy," he said, and that was the first time that my heart swelled with pride. The next was when he asked for the same shirt, with his name across the back, and some shin pads. I was falling into the trap of buying all the equipment possible, just like the pushy parents. We came out with cones, a mini-goal and even some Under Armour kit because he'd once seen me wearing it on a visit to the training ground.

Where we live, football is not a sport that one encourages one's offspring to participate in. Because of that there are no local teams, so we had to venture to the nearest big town, where the kids are very streetwise and wary of anybody different coming into their midst. If I'm honest, I've tried to shield my kids from this to a certain extent, because I didn't want them mixing with the kind of crowd that I used to mix with. All I've succeeded in doing, however, is alienating us from where we came from as well as from where we are now. We get the cold shoulder at my son's private school and at the flashy club round the corner, but just when I think that we should return to our roots, a mate will call to tell me that there was a spate of burglaries and a stabbing back home over the weekend.

I tracked down a local club that had decent facilities and was run by an ex-player; he explained that the boys were competitive but mostly just loved playing football. That was good enough for us and my son seemed to join in with the training sessions pretty well. The other kids bonded with him because they weren't born with silver spoons in their mouths and were very genuine, and my son loved the fact that these kids were actually talking to him. It was humbling to watch and made me feel like a piece of shit for what I'd asked him to become when we moved to our present home.

After a couple of weeks the coach said that he felt my son had enough about him to play in a match, and asked him to come along on Saturday. My son's first-ever football match! Suddenly I felt incredibly competitive. What if he was no good? What if he embarrassed himself? The other parents on the touchline would be looking at me wondering why my son, of all the kids there, couldn't play football.

We worked all week in the back garden and I tried not to come across as busy as Lewis Hamilton's dad, who uses the royal "we" when talking about his son's Formula One career. We practised passing, running with the ball, control – all the basic things – until his big day arrived. I was a bag of nerves but my son was very calm. As we drove down to the recreation pitches, past the burnt-out cars and the police chalk outlines on the ground, I pulled out a bottle of Lucozade and handed it to him.

"Quick, drink this," I said.

"I don't like Lucozade," he pointed out.

"Daddy drinks it," I said.

"OK, Daddy. Maybe just a bit, then."

We pulled into the car park and he jumped out and ran into the changing rooms. A few minutes later he emerged in his own little kit, the sleeves dangling over his hands. The coach spotted me and strolled over to tell me that my son was starting the game. I broke out in a sweat and my heart began to race. There was a good crowd, maybe 100 people, and the referee and linesman actually had the proper kit on, rather than the dodgy tracksuits that a couple of volunteers might have worn. Suddenly this all looked very official and it occurred to me that I hadn't given my son any advice whatsoever. How could I have let him go out there without warning him what to look out for? I'd short-changed my own flesh and blood.

The teams were lining up and the referee was checking with his linesman that they were ready to start. Then he set the timer on his watch. This is what we do at professional level. Did they realise the age of these kids? Jesus, was that a scout on the far side? I began to scrutinise the touchline for a man with a worn-out coat and a notepad, who would talk briefly to the coaches before getting into a crappy old car and driving off.

This was unbearable. He was going to be eaten alive out there. I had to get a message to him; I had to say something that would inspire him and encourage him to really get stuck in and cover up all the flaws in his game. He'd only been practising for two weeks! Surely people would take that into consideration, wouldn't they? I'd have to tell everyone, I decided. I'd have to go down the line and tell people once the game kicked off – the parents, the coaches. I'd have my son's back.

As the teams got ready and the referee put his arm in the air and the whistle to his lips, my mind was racing. I couldn't think of anything to say! I was panicking: some inspirational words were needed, something that my son would remember as a point of reference in his interviews after he lifted the FA Cup at Wembley in 20 years' time. Then it came to me.

He was on the far side of the pitch, so I cupped my hands around my mouth and called over to him.

"HEY!" I shouted.

He looked over. "Yes, Dad?" he yelled back.

"JUST DON'T BE SHIT, OK?"

"OK, Daddy," he said.

Perfect. Just in the nick of time, too.

INDEX

(the initials TSF refer to The Secret Footballer)

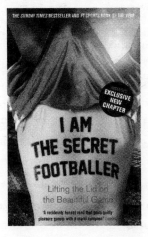